RIGHT TO PETITION

RIGHT TO PETITION

A Practical Guide to Creating Change in Government
with Political Advocacy Tools and Tips

NICOLE TISDALE

gatekeeper press

Columbus, Ohio

Right to Petition: A Practical Guide to Creating Change in
Government with Political Advocacy Tools and Tips

Published by Gatekeeper Press
2167 Stringtown Rd, Suite 109
Columbus, OH 43123-2989
www.GatekeeperPress.com

Library of Congress Control Number: 2019934904

ISBN (hardcover): 9781642375763
ISBN (paperback): 9781642375770
eISBN: 9781642375787

Printed in the United States of America
2

For my family and friends:
Thank you for your continuous and relentless support and encouragement. None of my ideas have ever been too much or too outlandish. There are no words for the love I have and support I feel from all of you. Thank you.

For every child from Nettleton, Mississippi:
I know the idea that "anything is possible" feels impossible to be true, but it is. There is nothing wrong with taking help when you need it; just remember to pay it forward when you can. Focus on out running your dreams. Then, dream new ones.

For Advocates, Members of Congress, and Staffers:
Your service, your work, and your strength are noticed and appreciated. Thank you. Keep fighting for good.

TABLE OF CONTENTS

INTRODUCTION

How Did I Get Here? My Story.

When I applied to law school, I told a room full of admissions lawyers that I didn't want to be a lawyer. What I wanted was to learn about public policy first, then law. I thought going to law school would be necessary for me to be a good policy expert.

A little background: I was approaching my senior year as an undergrad, with four or five political internships under my belt. And, like many ambitious 22-year-olds, I knew exactly what I was going to do for the rest of my life to impact the world.

I had interned in Washington, D.C., at a prestigious lobbying firm. I'd also spent time interning for a U.S. Senator in his Mississippi home office. I'd interned at local political offices, city halls, and campaigns. By this point, I wasn't just guessing that I didn't want to pursue my childhood dream of becoming a lawyer anymore—I was 100% sure I didn't want to be a lawyer.

I wanted to be a lobbyist.

I learned about lobbyists my freshman year at Ole Miss in a political science class. Until that point, I'd wanted to be an attorney. But when someone explained that a lobbyist goes to D.C. and represents people from home to help them get laws changed, I thought that was the perfect alternative to becoming a lawyer.

Clearly, I had a very green understanding of what it was to be a lobbyist.

In my personal statement to the law school, I explained why I wanted to be a lobbyist. I explained that I felt people didn't understand how laws were applied or interpreted in a courtroom. And I needed to be in the legislative branch so that I could have an impact on how bills are written, how messages are communicated, and how bills are explained to constituents during the legislative process. Law

1

school was a means to an end because there wasn't a graduate program anywhere for lobbyists.

Despite my personal statement (or maybe because of it), I got into law school. As it turns out, they really do consider the whole package. Plus, I'm sure my aggressively hard class curriculum, high GPA, and academic accolades didn't hurt. The University of Mississippi (Ole Miss) Law School took a chance on me. While I was there, I continued to find and excel in political internships. I took all the legislative and administrative law classes I could find. And by the time I graduated law school in 2009, in the middle of a financial recession, I had already landed a job on Capitol Hill.

I was going to work for one of the most prestigious and newest House committees: The House Committee on Homeland Security. The committee was led by a Mississippi Member of Congress whom I'd admired since Ms. Snow's fourth-grade history class—Chairman Bennie Thompson. This was a great opportunity, and I was beyond excited and grateful! Chairman Thompson took a chance on me.

Still, the reason I was working on the committee was that, ultimately, I was going to be a lobbyist. Like many staffers, I had a plan: Come to the Hill for three to five years, get a Rolodex/phone full of contacts, push some bills through Congress, and then become a lobbyist.

Here's the thing: Even though I was the queen of internships and volunteer organizations, I never anticipated how much I would love being a public servant as my full-time career. I didn't know how much I would enjoy solving problems for people, and most importantly, how much I would enjoy teaching people about the political process through our committee, our offices, and members of Congress.

And so my three-to-five-year plan turned into, "Three years really isn't enough time on the Hill."

Then, "Well I JUST got vested at five years. Plus, there are still some things I need to do. I'll leave in six years."

Then, "Seven years is more of a round number. I'll leave in seven years."

"Seriously, I'm leaving in nine . . ."

And at some point, I looked up and I had a decade of public service under my belt. And I realized that, not only were advocates and constituents coming to me for advice on how to get things done, but lobbyists were coming to me, too. Other staffers depended on me to explain things to them. Even Members of Congress sought me out as a policy confidante because I had been successful on the Hill, and because I'd become a teacher who could explain how others could do it, too. And of course, they still do.

Advocating and teaching people to advocate for themselves allows me to help thousands, maybe millions of people. That's why I needed to be on Capitol Hill.

How Can I Serve You?

One of the reasons I've stayed on the Hill is because every day I see people struggling with the politics, processes, and procedures of Congress. I see people with the best of intentions, but they don't know who to talk to, they're not making the best proposals, or they're not presenting their proposals well. And inevitably people get discouraged because they don't think that they're succeeding, and they don't know how to change things.

My goal as a staffer—and I work in an office that not only encourages this of all staff but requires it—is to help people understand how Congress can work for them. So, in our office, we never give a "no" followed by a period. Our "no" comes with a comma. When we do tell people, "No, we can't do X for you," we finish by saying, "But here are a number of other things we can do for you that are more helpful for your cause. Let me explain." The country girl in me calls that, "Giving folks a slow maybe instead of a fast no."

One reason I authored this book is because I fundamentally believe that the government operates only by the will and the voice of its people—and that's you.

Who Needs This Book?

My primary goal in this book is to empower you, through education, about the types of things you can petition your government for. I believe that providing the proper motivation and practical tools will teach you how to "fish" for your causes and communities on Capitol Hill. I want you to have success on the Hill beyond me, my office, and my time there.

My job on Capitol Hill has been giving people fish every day. I love that about my job. But this book is my way of teaching you how to fish.

This book is for those of you who have never had a member of Congress or staffer sit down and explain how this world really works. This book is for everyone who has gotten a no instead of an explanation of why the "ask" you are making isn't the best ask and what you should be asking for instead.

This book is your reference to use and grow your issues beyond me. Learn from it, put it to use, and educate your community. This book is for everyone who believes that they are in charge of their government. This book is for beginner activists and advocates who have decided that enough is enough. Those of you who have realized that there is a world around you that you are not involved in, but you know you should be.

This book is also for people who have already been active in their political and civic organizations. You pay your dues, you fundraise, you organize: you are already a grassroots advocate. You may even participate in fly-in days into D.C. and advocate to Members of Congress.

This book is also for people who may just end up having an opportunity to talk to your member of Congress, whether that be at a grocery store or gas station, a school event for your child, or a medical facility for a loved one.

Your Political Science 202 Class

This book is also for people who are looking for the steps to take after the protest. After your rally. After your march. This book is Political Science 202. While I will not use overly confusing terms and jargon, I assume that you already know the branches of government and that the legislative branch is the one you want to target, or the place where you want to focus a portion of your messaging and advocacy efforts.

I will not be explaining how Members of Congress are elected or how to get a job on Capitol Hill. I am also not going to explain how a bill becomes a law. Hint: *School House Rock!* still has the best and most comprehensive three-minute explanation out there. I'm also not going to explain how to write a letter or email or start a Twitter storm to get the attention of your Member of Congress – there are already several books on this. Besides, that's not my area of expertise. I'm a Capitol Hill staffer who understands congressional advocacy.

Far from the cutthroat image many have of Washington, the congressional community is very collegial and cooperative. We help each

4

other. If you could sit with a staffer for three hours, they would share with you much of what is in this book.

I've looked for other books like this. And I embarked on this journey because I couldn't find them. I struggled with where to send people when they came into our office and needed help developing political strategies. If there was a book that had this info in it, I would have read it before coming to Capitol Hill, and so would have every staffer. In this book, I present the information I couldn't find. You deserve this information.

This book is meant to inspire you and prepare you for your political advocacy journey. I'm here to remind you that you can't afford to sit this out. I'm going to say aloud what you need to hear: We actually do need you to tell us what's going on in our communities, as much as you need us to help you change what's happening.

As an attorney, a staffer, a constituent, and a lifelong cheerleader, my goal is for you to use this book as a guide for all your political advocacy with the legislative branch. This book can be used by policy advocates, grassroots activists, government affairs professionals, journalists, students, professors, librarians, and anyone who has a complaint or a cause before the federal government. This book is also for Members of Congress, staffers, and interns. Whether you have been in the legislative branch for 30 years or 30 minutes, there are always things we can learn about being better public servants. We're all still learning with each other and from each other.

How Do You Use This Book?

Some of you may pick up this book and read it from cover to cover in one sitting. Some of you may get into a few chapters and realize there are some things you want to tackle before advocating before Congress, so you'll just mark pages to come back to later. Others may read a few chapters and think this is the cure for insomnia. All of those would be fair actions and opinions because this book is a political advocacy reference book.

I have no flights of fancy about this book. You're not likely to curl up by the fire with it or lie out by the pool with it. This book is designed to be your resource when you need it. I want it to be the guide you come back to time and time again. The margins are extra wide so you can take notes. You can dog-ear pages or fold them down completely.

I encourage you to highlight until your markers run dry. The guide is full of stories, tips, tools, and insider's information. Use what you need now and save other information for later.

Develop an ear for complaints. When you hear a student, friend, neighbor, or colleague rant or gripe about something, recognize it as an opportunity to advise and teach them how to turn a complaint into a plan. Come back to the book. Help identify an advocacy tool to help.

When you use one political advocacy tool, come back to the book for another one. If a tool does not work, come back to the book. Take more notes. Highlight more words. As you read a passage and get an idea, write it down. It may not be a crucial tool for you right now, and maybe you can't use it today. But in six months or a year, it may be just the tool you need to jumpstart you and your issue to success.

Let's Wrap This Up.

In conclusion, I'm going to be your personal guide to political advocacy in Congress. While I hope that I'll be able to meet as many of you as possible in person, I know better. Now that I'm coming up on a decade of public service in Congress, the most important lesson I have learned is that a good public servant touches and helps people they will never meet. That's also what good public policy does.

Good public policy is not something you can always see immediate results from. But good public policy will produce better and healthier communities. I say that as a graduate of Head Start. Someone was on Capitol Hill in the early 60s, decades before I was born, advocating for educational funding opportunities for low-income families and low-income children. As I sit here today with a couple of college degrees and several accolades, writing and independently publishing a book, I know that the advocates and public policy for children like me are the reason that I am in a place to serve you, write for you, and teach you. I hope I can help you too.

Now Let's Do This!

This book is divided into two sections: preparing for success, Part I, and the advocacy asks, Part II. There are a few concepts that you will need to master in Chapter 1. In Chapter 2, I will show you how to be politically grounded and smart about your issue. For instance, how relevant is your issue to the person you are asking for help? In Chapter 3, we'll talk about how to build relationships on the Hill or off the Hill the smart way, including understanding people, their motivations, and having respect for their work.

In Chapter 4, we will dig into the mistakes or roadblocks that trip people up the most so that you can avoid them. Once you have those under your belt, you'll be ready to choose and construct your advocacy ask. I will give you the background, the openings, and the closings that we staffers wish to hear from everyone who comes to our offices. In Chapter 5, I will show you how to create a proposal that will get an answer of "Yes."

Moving on to Part 2, in Chapter 6, I'll explain how to use the 40+ political advocacy tools I will give you. And then finally, in Chapters 7 through 9, you will find over 40 advocacy ask tips and how to make them work for your issue or your organization.

Ultimately, it is important for me to teach you that we, as insiders and as staffers, can help you if you help us. In fact, we *want* to help you. And I'm thrilled that this book is one of the first of its kind. I look forward to teaching you how to advocate for yourself before Congress.

PART I
PREPARE FOR SUCCESS

CHAPTER 1

Mindset: Petitioning is like Farming.

I grew up on a farm in Mississippi and one of my favorite things to eat was strawberries. I ate them whole, cold, fresh, in preserves, and canned (in jars). There was one problem with strawberries in the south: they only grew in the summer. Everyone in my family explained this to me, and I even had a couple of standoffs with the manager (my friend's dad) at the Piggly Wiggly when they didn't have strawberries. I was well aware of how growing seasons worked, but I was stubborn and wanted strawberries year-round.

So, I did what any know-it-all eight-year-old would do—I decided to grow my own strawberries. Then I could eat fresh strawberries whenever I wanted! It was the perfect plan. I tried growing them in containers on kitchen window sills and by our hot-water heater. Because summers in Mississippi feel like showers in terms of heat and humidity, I tried growing strawberries in our bathroom. I tried to grow strawberries everywhere. Naturally, all of my plans were epic fails. For those two years, my family, especially our resident farmer—Uncle Bubba—just watched and waited for me to learn what they already knew: You have to do what you can when you can, but it takes time, patience, and rationale to see your efforts grow.

What do strawberries have to do with advocating on Capitol Hill? You have to be patient and realistic, listen to folks who have toiled before you, and work within the process to produce the results you want. This may not be what you want to hear. But, like strawberries, everything has a natural rhythm and season. Things may not happen when you want them to. Politics are no different.

When it comes to government and politics, all of us want something done. And we all want it done yesterday. But you're here for a reason, and you're trying to figure out your season. It could be that you are frustrated with what you see happening or not happening in Congress. Maybe you've always focused your efforts on the Executive Branch and found that those efforts could be severely hampered by whoever was in the White House. You could be concerned about the direction of your community. On the positive side, your government may have gotten something right, and you don't want it stripped away or repealed.

Whatever strategy you've been using, I'm sure you recognize that where government is involved, the situation will not change overnight; you understand you've got to wait on your strawberries to grow.

Petitioning the government also has seasons. There will be summers for your issue when everyone is interested, everyone will look to you as an expert, and you're going to see movement. But there will also be winters for your issue, when you may feel invisible, or that people aren't concerned with the issues like they should be. But winter doesn't mean that there isn't anything happening. There are simply different tools that you should be using in the winter to grow your strawberries than you used in the summer to pick your strawberries.

A season change doesn't mean that you should give up. You need winter political advocacy tools and summer political advocacy tools. There are things that you can do in the "growing season" and outside it to advance your issue.

This book describes the process of petitioning. It gives you clarification and inside information on how Capitol Hill really works.

This book will not teach you to hunt. You cannot just read the book and get a bill passed next Monday. If that's your goal, this is not the book for you. But if you're willing to change your approach, then this book will be a valuable resource.

Political advocacy is a long-term process, like farming. You have to plant seeds and tend the field. Later, possibly a long time after planting, you'll reap the benefits. This book will teach you how to farm on Capitol Hill.

You're Right to Petition

Petitioning is nothing more than participating in our democracy. It's a necessity. The voice of the people shows the government what needs to be done. You owe it to yourself, to your family, and to your community to get involved. Petitioning is your First Amendment right. If you're not currently participating in our democracy, you should be.

Imagine this: What if we lived in a world where political advocates didn't exist? What if there were no advocates to make an ask? What if there was no accountability for our government? What would happen? If this scenario does not end in complete chaos, you're not imagining it correctly.

Ultimately, our government represents us and our needs. Still, some people choose not to participate. Some people say they don't really like politics, that politics are too polarizing, or that they just don't "do politics." I always tell them, "If you choose not to participate, you only make it easier for people to make decisions for you." You can't afford not to participate.

Civic participation in democracy is more than voting. Voting is merely the first step. The next step is following up, which involves keeping your Members of Congress accountable, reminding them of what you need, and getting answers from them about how they are serving you and your communities.

In this book, I'm going to discuss petitioning, and I'll use the term interchangeably with advocating or advocacy. But I don't want you to get hung up on the words. It's all about communicating with Congress, no matter what you call it.

The good news is, nothing in this book requires any new or special skills. What you need is something that you already have: the ability to connect with other people. The ability to tell your story and express what's important to you and why. No one can tell your story like you can. Members of Congress and their staffers, like me, want to hear from you and to help you.

But Nobody Has Taught Us How to Petition

In the past, you may have run into some barriers to petitioning the government. The first one is that no one has taught you how to petition. You don't quite know how to make the change you want. People tell me all the time, "I must've missed this class," or maybe, "I slept through this class." The truth is, no one taught us how to advocate in school.

People who don't know how to petition usually say one of three things: they don't know where to start, they don't know how to interact with government officials to make change in Congress, or they don't know how to make their voices heard as one of many.

Let's address the first problem: not knowing where to start. I'm going to give you information on starting with a new member of Congress and with one who has been in for 26 years, whether it's your first day as an advocate, or your 500th day, or your 50th year.

Start at home and figure out what's most important to you. Then this book will show you how to build from there. I won't push you to go from zero to ten overnight. If you are at zero, this book will get you to a solid one or two. Then, in a year, you'll look back and realize that you've been using several of these tips and tools, and you'll find yourself at a nine or ten, and you'll keep on building. This book is a building block, and it should be used as such.

The second obstacle I will address is not knowing how to interact with members of Congress and staffers in order to make changes. This book goes way beyond your high school civics or college political science classes. It's not only the accumulation of my ten years working on Capitol Hill, but also the decades and centuries of service that other staffers have shared with me.

The third obstacle is not knowing how to make yourself heard when you feel your voice is one among many. The truth is, you *are* one voice among many. But I'll show you how to distinguish yourself, and what not to do when you come to Capitol Hill. The foundation of petitioning is based on developing relationships, and I'm going to give you some tips on how to do it.

Other people tell me that petitioning has a steep learning curve, that the Hill is overwhelming, and that we use too much jargon and confusing lingo. Yes, like any other profession, we have unique processes and jargon that may be unfamiliar to you. The truth is, though, that some people may be using overly technical terms on purpose to confuse you and restrict your participation. I hate when people put up those barriers. I will talk to you in plain language, using everyday terms and stories, because I want you to master this information and be able to put it into action.

I know that Capitol Hill is intimidating. I've seen some of the biggest celebrities, the top athletes, the richest CEOs end up a nervous wreck, with voices quivering throughout our meetings. But it doesn't have to be that way. Once you accept that everyone has to go through Capitol Hill, and every important issue comes this way, advocacy gets easier.

Yes, there are very smart, very rich people advocating next to you on the Hill. But they're not your competition. The worst-kept secret in D.C. is that the most important people are the constituents — that is, the people who vote members of Congress into and out of office. Those people are you.

If you're feeling intimidated, try going in with a David-and-Goliath, Grasshopper-and-Ant, or Tortoise-and-Hare attitude. Know that there will be lots of flashy, important-seeming or self-important people around you, but they aren't always the most impactful. You can be Jane Doe from nowhere and still make an impact, no matter your background.

The Hill is cut out for tortoises. Hares do not stay in Congress very long because hares make impulsive decisions, hares take impulsive votes, and hares don't think about real action.

Hares do not make good staffers either. Staffers must be analytical and deliberate with their work and their recommendations to members of Congress. Moreover, staffers don't like hares coming into our offices because they rush us, and they don't allow us to be deliberate and thoughtful.

Both staffers and members of Congress must work steadily, like tortoises. That's how members of Congress get elected and that's how staffers get and keep their jobs. We all work for Congress, and we are all farming.

Aside from the intimidation factor, many people feel they need special skills to get involved. I'm an attorney, but I always remind people that coming to Capitol Hill is not like going into a courtroom where you need a special degree or must be an experienced attorney. It's also not like going into an operating room where you need to be a licensed doctor.

Instead, when you come to Capitol Hill, remember that you're talking to your neighbor. These are the people who live where you live, have worked where you work, and are doing their best to represent you. They didn't need to be special to run for office, and you don't need special skills to talk to them.

That said, there are some things you can do to be a more effective communicator, and I'll teach you many of those things. But there are no prerequisites for your learning. You can be effective using the skills you already have. You might be thinking, "Sure, she thinks I have the skills, but I don't." Okay, if you don't have any of the skills in this book, just say, "Hi."

You can use this book to learn the purpose of these tools and then form your own ideas for the legislative process, based on what you are capable of and what you think will work for you. I only ask that, if you create a new political advocacy tool and come to the Hill to use it with members of Congress and staff, you email me about your new tool. I'm always looking to learn!

Seeds Don't Sprout Overnight

I see people coming to the Hill and shooting themselves and their issue in the foot all the time. I can't say it enough: just as farming takes seasons, political advocacy takes time. People come in frustrated with Congress because they are deadlocked on issues that are important to them. Some of them feel that Congress just doesn't care.

When you come to the Hill with that negative thought process and negative energy, you bring it into your meetings. You can't hide it, and we can see it. That attitude makes it hard for us to work with you and make the most of our limited time together. You should know that we do care. Often, we just need to be properly informed, but we have limited time and a lot of issues to address.

Also, petitioners are often unrealistic about the results that they can achieve. I've had people come in who think that we can get an entire bill drafted, introduced through the committee process, approved through the chambers, and bring it into public law in a matter of months. They think that a person can come to the Hill for one visit and be done. That's not true. You must keep in mind that the issues that matter to you have a massive impact on communities, on the future of our country, and on the livelihood of our planet. They all require thoughtful debate and policy considerations.

There is no magic trick to solving huge social and political issues. They're too complex. They impact people all over the world. Public policy problem-solving takes a lot of work and a lot of time.

In addition to not being realistic about the results, sometimes people are not specific enough in what they ask. I'll give you more than 40 tools so that you can ensure that once you have a realistic expectation, you also have a realistic ask. See Part II for the series of political advocacy asks or tools.

One challenge is that, as a petitioner, you don't have much time on Capitol Hill. But petitioning is a long game, so you need to make the most of the time that you have in the places where you are. There are efficient uses of your time, and then there are things that may seem like they're helping but just slow you down or kill time. I will show you where to focus, how to focus, and how to increase your yield.

How to Increase Your Yield

The key to creating change in government is to build momentum. It's very rare for a bill to become an instant bill or an instant law. We have seen almost instant laws after terrible events like 9/11, Hurricane Katrina, Watergate, the 2008 recession, and the subsequent auto bailout. So if you hear that something became law overnight, it's not true. There are no overnight celebrities, and there are no overnight laws. To build momentum, you need to move forward in steps. In farming, you plant seeds, you tend the field, you harvest the crops, and you do it again next year. The cycle continues.

Petitioning is similar in that someone needs to start the chain, and someone needs to continue what has gone before. Someone has to reach out to Congress to plant the seeds, which means educating the members. You tend the field by building relationships with members of Congress. You harvest the crops by gaining publicity and getting a movement behind your issue. And then, you need to do it again and again, year after year.

You are a part of the process. You are just as much a farmer in the political process as a member of Congress or a staffer. Success comes from forging personal relationships with an office and then making a reasonable and relevant request. I'll show you exactly what you need to understand so that you can help others while you petition.

CHAPTER 2

Prepare: Be Politically Grounded

Success comes from making asks that are reasonable and relevant. To do this you need to be politically grounded. The word "political" means much more than just votes and debates. Being politically grounded involves many of the same thought processes you use in your everyday life. Allow me to illustrate this point with a true story about what **not** to do when meeting your member of Congress.

Once, a group of farmers came into our office on a fly-in day. A fly-in day is when a large group of advocates comes to the Hill at the same time. They are organized mainly by their Congressional districts and states. Ideally, at least one person in the group should be a constituent of the member of Congress they are meeting. It may be the only time that year that they will meet their member of Congress, so the most important thing they can offer is a connection to home.

These farmers came at a time when the most-discussed issue on the Hill was the Farm Bill, a huge undertaking for all of us. They were also interested in issues related to national security, which is my area of expertise. Why were farmers interested in this topic? They were concerned about biodefense. There are few issues on the Hill that do not touch other subject matters.

I arrived at the meeting early. Members typically run behind schedule due to votes and other meetings, but here's a tip: when a member is running late, have at least one person from your group stay to wait for them. Members do not advertise this, but if you came all the way to D.C. for a 30-minute meeting with them, they will give you their time and full attention, even if they are behind schedule. My boss does this because he doesn't believe in cutting people short. But you must stay in the office to receive this courtesy.

This delegation of farmers came from Mississippi, some from my part of Mississippi. I sat in the lobby talking to them as we waited for my boss. He was late, and they had another meeting with a different senator, scheduled for soon after, so they had to decide who was going to stay and wait and who was going to leave.

One of the group members – let's call him Sam – was from my boss's district. While they were debating, I suggested to them that Sam should stay because the others might not understand some of the nuanced questions that would come up. But Sam also wanted to meet the senator. I watched them go back and forth and hoped they would take my advice, but they didn't. The one individual who was from the district, who had the closest connection and most familiarity with the member of Congress, left.

Meanwhile, my boss expected someone from his district to be at the meeting because we always give members advance briefs on the makeup of visiting groups. (That's why staffers ask you who is coming and from where). He arrived, shook everyone's hand, and asked, "Now, who's from Greenville?"

The visitors looked at each other and explained that the gentleman from Greenville had to leave because he wanted to meet one of the Mississippi senators.

My boss said, "So wait a minute. There was one person in the group that was from my district and y'all sent him away?" He chuckled. In that moment, they understood that they had made an unwise decision despite the nudge I had given them. I don't think they fully recovered their composure during that meeting.

I work for a nice, cordial Member of Congress. He was prepared to talk about some awfully specific issues with Sam, issues he'd heard about from other Greenville farmers. And he wanted to do what everyone does: play the name game and figure out who knows who, and whose kids went to school with whose kids, and whose grandkids are in school together now. He couldn't do this with anyone in the group who stayed.

You won't always have someone with you who has that kind of connection with a member of Congress. But when you do, it's important to take advantage of it. When I say this chapter is about being "politically grounded," it's really about thinking through all the politics of a strategy, including who is going to deliver your message.

This chapter will take you inside the head of a staffer and show the political decisions we make when we talk to members of Congress about issues. I'll take you through the thought process you, as an advocate, should have as you figure out the politics of your issue. Success comes from making reasonable and relevant connections and requests. Be aware of where you fit into the bigger picture of what is going on in Congress.

In the above example with the farmers, the group did not "fail," but they didn't do their best. Unless you do something egregious when coming to the Hill, you will not fail or be barred from meeting your legislator. But I want you to have a meeting where you feel you've gotten what you came for and have a plan for the next step, and where you know you've done all that you could do.

When you come to the Hill, you want to eliminate negative consequences by being prepared. This book will help you figure out your strategy until it becomes second nature, and you will end up as passionate about petitioning and advocacy as you are about your issue.

You'll need to know why the member should care about your issue, how it affects them, and how it connects to local and national issues. Here are four ways to be more politically grounded and speak from a position of strength:

1. Know your issue
2. Look for other members of Congress who will support your issue
3. Do the research on your member of Congress, their positions, and their party
4. Connect your member of Congress to the issue in question

Make Connections to Your Issue for Your Audience

Making connections between your issue and the member of Congress you wish to speak to is your job, not the staffers' and not the member's. These connections can be geographical (you worked at a factory in his district), personal (the member of Congress is a former teacher, and your issue is education reform), or political (you know your legislator supports a similar issue). Later, we will discuss what to do if your legislator is opposed to your issue.

Recently, a group came in to talk to the Homeland Security Committee about some cyber workforce issues and how they wanted to grow the cyber workforce. They referred to a comprehensive report on the issue, and I said, "Oh, this is the same report that said Jackson,

Mississippi, has the least diverse cyber workforce and the lowest numbers of any major city in the United States."

Though we were talking about the same report, they had forgotten they were talking to people who worked for a member who represents the city of Jackson. They missed an opportunity to connect with us over that talking point and statistic. We were already familiar with the report and the daunting statistic from Jackson, but what if we hadn't been? This would have been a wonderful way to get us interested in the issue at hand, as connected as it was to the member of Congress's.

Create the narrative for your audience. Explain why they should care about the issue and why it is important. Over time, if you do this well, you will turn them into advocates of your issue too.

Watch out for trigger words such as "important." If you use such qualifying adjectives, you need to be prepared for a member or staffer to ask you, "why?" You need to know the answer. Keep the "whys" in mind as you prepare your speech—the answers should lead to the best ways for you to build that connection between your issues and your member of Congress.

All politics is local. This phrase is constantly repeated on the Hill, but people forget. At some level, you must connect your issue to the 750,000 or more constituents your member of Congress represents. Think of this from the point of view of a member of Congress: He (using my boss as an example) works for his constituents, and any time he spends on an issue unconnected with those constituents is time he is not working for them. If any member of Congress spends more time working for other constituencies than for his own, he will not be in Congress long. So, to be heard and to get a positive response, make the connection between your issue and the member's constituents, and make it as early as possible.

TIP: Start at the Home Office before the D.C. Office.

A lot of people want to start with the Washington staff, but sometimes the best place to go is the local district office. The district staff, on average, has worked for the member longer than the D.C. staff. They are like the people the member entrusts with his home when he's away. These people travel around the district and the state meeting people, and they are among the most trusted and powerful staff for members of Congress.

Depending on what your ask is, the district staff may be in a better position to get it executed. And if they are not, their referral to the

D.C. office will mean a lot. This referral can take the form of calls or emails. If they redirect you to D.C., feel free to say, "Do you mind if I tell them that I reached out to you all and you referred me?" And of course, they will say that's fine. Alternatively, you can ask them to send an email connecting you to someone from the D.C. office. Most of the time, they will do so.

Start with the staff, often from the district—we staff can help you find a solution if you show us the problem. Keep in mind that the D.C. staff may not be plugged into the geographic or personal connections a member may have to the issue. They may not have even lived in that state or district. If you know about something, from institutional knowledge or because of some connections you have back home with the member, don't be afraid to tell the D.C. staff that.

Remember that these representatives you are meeting are people. A lot of the issues you speak to Congress about are people issues. Talk to them about how your issue affects their district, their state, the nation, and the global community. Public servants are problem solvers. They are happiest when they are fixing things or, as Southern people say, "earning their keep."

Know Your Issue

Knowing your issue means being able to explain it in the most succinct, elevator-pitch-but-the-door-is-about-to-open way possible. Many of the people who come to us think they are using the elevator pitch. I don't know what kind of elevators these people are on, but they take 15 minutes to explain their issue.

Our elevator doors close quickly in Congress. You need to introduce your issue, outline your problem, and explain its current status, all quickly. Try to fit each of those into one or two sentences. We will have a conversation later, and we can dive deeper then.

Geek out on your issue. Prepare the stats: the number of people the issue affects, how funding has decreased (or not increased enough) over the years, etc. Highlight which stats are the most compelling.

TIP: Test out your stats on other people first.

If you tell someone that one third of constituents are impacted by an issue, that's interesting. But saying that 233,000 people are affected may be more compelling. Put on your sales hat and figure out how to explain these stats in a way that's less "Bill Nye the Science Guy" and more "Oprah motivational." Not all stats are compelling. That doesn't mean they are not important, but don't use them if they don't serve your purpose.

TIP: Keep a running list of powerful stats you come across.

Later, I will talk about attaching stories to those stats. We staffers keep a master list of statistics by topic and pull them out as we need them, adjusting them for use at a press conference, a member's floor statement, or a graduation speech.

Evaluate the status of your advocacy issues. Are people you know mobilized and passionate, and do you want your member of Congress to know? Tell them about the recent rally with 100 people. Or are you concerned because people do not yet know there is lead in the water, and you need to push and publicize this?

If you're struggling to come up with what has been done, it's a good time to evaluate what you are doing. Open a Google spreadsheet and make a list: rallies, dates, attendance, fliers. We keep these documents for members. They will ask us about conferences they have attended, and we can look in our files and say, "You went two years ago and there were about 100 people." We can even pull up the speeches that were given.

As you see, some of the techniques I'm suggesting are the same systems that staffers and members of Congress use. They work.

Know the legislative history and state of current laws on your issue. Is there anything happening in Congress now regarding your issue? And remember that you cannot come to the Hill and talk to members of Congress about an issue on the national level if you haven't done your homework on what's going on at the state and local level. Because they will.

After all, there's a running joke that every member of Congress wants to always know *everything* that is going on in their city and state. If they had not been involved in the politics of their city and state, they wouldn't have been voted into their present positions. Though legislators themselves, they are also the constituents of their state legislature and of the mayor of their city. So, it's not that these members are uninformed. They may just need to be reminded of certain issues and refreshed on how they came about.

So, make sure you know what's happening in your member of Congress's backyard. A national issue probably became national after something happened at the local or state level. If you want to have credibility and work effectively, you need to know as much (if not more) about your issue as the person you will be speaking with. Even if you just say something like, "I know the Farm Bill is going to be up next month" (or in six months). It's perfectly fine to estimate the timing of bills if you don't know. We often don't know anything concrete until it's heading to the floor, but you will have a friend for life if you can tell us something we haven't heard.

If possible, connect your issue to current events. Are you talking about veterans' issues near Veterans Day? Have there recently been school closings, and you want to talk about education funding? Use relevant connections if you have them, but don't force them.

These are some of the things you should be thinking of when preparing your petition. In Chapter 4, I will show you how to edit your message into its most concentrated form.

Know Your Members of Congress

You may have heard that the most wonderful sound to a person is their name, but to members of Congress and their staff, the second-most wonderful sound is the name of their hometown. You don't need to know where every staffer is from, but you should know the member's hometown. My boss comes from a small town. He still lives there, used to be the mayor, and still has his district office there. Most members, though they may move around, are proud of their hometown. Even if you have never been to their hometown, at least acknowledge that you've heard of it.

And don't pretend to know these facts—learn them! Most people do not personally know their member of Congress, so don't worry if you don't. But you should never try to build a relationship on fake connections and familiarity. We will pick up on it.

As an aside, I'll never run for office because I am bad with names and faces. No one would vote for me twice because every time they saw me, I'd be introducing myself and asking for their support. Most members of Congress have gotten the hundreds of thousands of people in their district to vote for them because they have great memories when it comes to names, faces, or traits. The best ones can remember all three. So, if you don't know a Member of Congress, don't pretend that you do. Acknowledge the fact and do your homework.

Why is this important? I'm trying to teach you to build trust with your member of Congress. Half-truths may get you through one meeting, but when the truth comes out, everything will crumble. Members and their staff have memories like elephants when it comes to people who have lied to them, and that information will be passed down to new staffers.

Lying can get you blackballed from an office or, worse, we may meet with you—not to help you but to show you to other staffers as a warning. I may tell the staffer, for example, "We're going to meet with John. John is not to be trusted with information about X and Y. Any time he gives you information, you need to check it and identify another source." That's the death penalty equivalent, and it does happen, but only for the most egregious offenses.

The fact that you're reading this book means you're not a John. As long as you are truthful, you don't have to worry about being blackballed.

You can use the social media pages for Members of Congress to find personal connections and collect conversation fodder. Know some basic information, such as where they went to college, or if they've been traveling recently? They may also have community groups listed on social media.

If you were unable to do this research, just note whether they are drinking coffee or Coke. My boss can talk for three or four minutes about his Southern Pecan coffee, which he loves and brings with him from Mississippi. I'm amazed at the number of people who come into our office who also love Southern Pecan coffee even though they might not be from the South. I often have to interrupt their coffee-talk and remind them to discuss the policy issues!

Remember that members of Congress are human beings who want to make a connection, and a personal connection is often the quickest and most effective.

Don't assume that, because an issue is important to you, it must be important to your member of Congress. Find out why a particular member might care about an issue—they may have lost a loved one to cancer or have to drive on highways that are in disrepair.

TIP: **Start with a high-level web search.** When a new member is coming to Congress, or when seeking members who can help with an issue, staffers do a general web search. Put the member's first and last name in quotation marks along with a plus or comma and your issue (e.g., "Nicole Tisdale + labor unions"). Sort by most recent and scan at a high level. That's the easiest way to find your member's view on an issue. If your legislator has a common name, add their title to the search (outside the quotation marks).

If you are participating in a fly-in and expect to meet a lot of members in a lot of delegations, you may not have time to research all of them. Focus on the ones within your district and state. You're not responsible for knowing everything about everyone. Research just strengthens your chances of success.

TIP: Check their press releases on their congressional and campaign websites. Enter the keywords for your issue, and you may find out that, for example, their spouse is a cancer survivor. Don't forget that congressional and campaign websites are separate. After a member of Congress is elected, they will still maintain their campaign website since they'll need it again. Also, remember to check event press centers for press releases.

When building political connections, many advocates do their homework backward: they focus on the member of Congress's position in the national party and with the president. But you need to start from the bottom and work up. Start with the state delegation and the committees and caucuses they may be part of, and then look at the national party. The last thing you should think about is their relationship to the president—your member of Congress is part of the legislative branch of government, not the executive branch, and there is a natural and purposeful tension between those branches.

State Delegations: The state delegation involves the relationships the member has with their two senators and the other representatives from their state. Regardless of the member's party affiliation, when the state delegation is doing well, it's good for everyone in that circle. It never hurts a state delegation for a member to be the chairwoman or a ranking member of a committee. It's even better if that ranking member belongs to your party, but ultimately, when a state wins, everyone in it wins. If a new factory opens up in District 1, workers from Districts 2 and 3 will commute there, and it will stimulate the economy. And those benefits will spread throughout the state and, sometimes, the region.

I work for the only Democratic legislator from Mississippi, but he is the chairman of the U.S. House Committee on Homeland Security, which handles cyber issues. On the Senate side, a Republican senator from Mississippi chairs the Commerce Committee, which also handles cyber issues. So, guess which state delegation is going to be hyper-focused on bipartisan, bicameral cyber issues?

That does not mean that the top Republican and the top Democrat from my state will agree on *every* issue. But within that delegation, they will work together on pushing our state forward.

Committees: Members of Congress end up on committees because they want to be there. At the beginning of every Congress, members create their committee wish list, in which they explain why they would be a good fit for a particular committee and why they are passionate about the issues. As a petitioner, you need to know what committees they are on and their roles. Even if you think their committee's issues do not align with yours, there may be a niche area where they connect.

To learn what subcommittees and assignments your member of Congress is on, go to the committee's website and search for the member's last name. You can then find out what they have been doing for that committee. Or you can go to the member's website and search for the committee name or topic. You may find that a member has a tense relationship with a committee. They may have marked up a bill or opposed a bill that the committee ended up passing.

TIP: You are not responsible for knowing the full history of what a member has done, or her committee involvement. Instead, I suggest looking at the committee assignments as they stand now and then going back one Congressional session (two years).

TIP: Search for your issue. If you're not finding results in your search, try broadening it. If "cancer research funding" yields no relevant results, try "cancer."

TIP: For example, "Ways and Means" does not have the word "health" in it, so most people do not know it's the committee that deals with health care. (See Bonus Materials for a classification of committee authorities and jurisdictions.)

Caucus: As with committees, if your member of Congress is in a caucus, she wants to be there because she has a connection with the issues. She has a connection with the other members. And she has decided to mobilize and publicize those connections.

A lot of caucuses involve niche issues that members care about. There is a caucus on unmanned aerial drones. Its members will be the most active, interested, and knowledgeable people on the Hill about drones. They have taken a purposeful action to join a caucus that focuses on that issue.

TIP: Check members' long bio for caucus memberships.

Wikipedia also does a decent job of listing caucus memberships for each member of Congress, and it's usually current. Even staffers use Wikipedia.

National Party: Your member of Congress may not be on the same page as their party on every issue, so don't just assume they are. At this time, the Democratic party in general opposes the proposed border wall. But you may not know the nuances of each member's position. Some are against it because they see it as a waste of money. Others may live near the border and believe the wall will create problems for animals and the environment. Some see it as a barrier to trade and international relationships. Make sure you understand your Congress member's individual views in relation to the party views.

Relative to the President: Find out where your member of Congress is in relation to the president, keeping in mind that tensions may exist between the legislative and executive branches. What I often do is search for the member's last name and the president's last name to find the last time they were together or whether the member has said anything negative or positive about the president, and vice versa.

Depending on where the member is with the president, you can play this up or down. For example, if your member of Congress supports the president on the border wall and you oppose it, it's probably best not to bring it up if you don't have to. If this is the issue you are speaking about, do not remind the member that they have already voiced their support for the wall publicly.

Their Personal Opinion: Keep in mind that very few members of Congress can take black-and-white positions on issues that fall into gray areas. They are representing some 750,000 constituents with different views. My boss, a Democrat, has held his seat for 25 years. That means that for 25 years the Republicans in his district have had a Democratic Member of Congress making votes on their behalf. He knows that, every two years, those Republicans are probably voting for his opponent. But he still represents all 750,000 constituents in Congress, not just the people who voted for him. Very few members of Congress run unopposed. They don't have the option of only representing the people who like them, and they have to make hard decisions.

TIP: Sign up for the newsletter from your Member of Congress, even if you don't support them or their party. You need to keep an eye

on what they are saying about your issues. This is even more important if they do not support your issue because you need to be able to
counter their arguments.

TIP: **If you can't find what you are looking for, ask.** Members
may even be grateful for the reminder to add more information to
their page.

Also, a Member of Congress may not have fully articulated positions on every issue. Use this to your advantage. A member of Congress may have an opinion that he has not stated publicly. You also
have an advantage here since it's easier for a member to reverse a private opinion than a public one.

If your member of Congress is not on the same side as you regarding your issue, but is not adamantly opposed to the issue, focus on
building the relationship. This may help you get a slow "maybe" rather
than a fast "no."

If you're struggling to connect your issue to your member of Congress, you may need a different audience. At some point, accept that
your legislator may never support your issue; otherwise, you may
waste valuable years trying to change their mind.

Know When to Reach Beyond Your Member of Congress

Staffers come from different constituencies and personal backgrounds. You can apply much of what you've learned about connecting with legislators to connect with the staffers you are scheduled to
meet. Learn about them and their positions on your issue (though
staffers are more difficult to research than members of Congress).

TIP: **Research, but don't cyberstalk.** Don't be a creep. You don't
need to know *everything* about us to connect. Just research enough to
facilitate a friendly conversation. You may end up in a meeting with
the subject matter expert and the communications team if you need
publicity for your issue. Talk to them about press-related events.

Try not to get caught up in the trap of trying to meet someone "important." All staffers, no matter their level, are the decision-makers for
their areas of responsibility. If you are in front of them, they're probably the right audience (see Bonus Materials for staff positions and duties). People who come in and want to meet the member or the chief
of staff don't realize that they will ask us later for recommendations on
what they should do about your issue.

Staffers are looking for promotions and want to be helpful. But they also remember people who snubbed them. The interns of today are the chiefs of staff of tomorrow. I came to the Hill in 2009 as an intern, and I now run a subcommittee of five people.

When I came to Washington, I was not yet a barred attorney. People came in asking to speak with "the attorneys" on maritime workers' security rights, my area of expertise. I told them I was responsible for the issue and offered to speak with them, but they were disappointed that I was the only a staffer in the meeting. What they didn't realize was that workers' security rights were one of the first issues I was responsible for, fresh out of law school, and I was trying to knock all my issues out of the park to impress my boss. It was important to me to do a great job, and I was the one pushing the committee to be more active on their issues. I was new, but I was the only person working on their issues. But none of that mattered to some people because they wanted to talk with a "counsel" or a "director."

Once I'd passed the bar and been sworn in, and my business card said "counsel" on it, guess who were the first people who wanted to meet with me? Of course, I met with them, but staffers do not forget people who treat them badly. It's a been a decade, and I'm bad with names, but I still remember the names of certain visitors and warn my colleagues about them.

Staffers are not petty, but we simply don't have time for people who are trying to filter us based on our titles. That's not the way the Hill works. Always defer to the offices about who you should be talking to. Demanding to talk to a certain person is an amateur move. Don't worry about the title. You want to speak with the person who is talking to your member of Congress about the issue you are interested in. You may want to talk to the chief of staff, but it may be best to develop a relationship with the legislative correspondent or legislative assistant who works on your issue.

TIP: Start with the staffers. You cannot get to most Members of Congress without first going through the staffers. If someone meets my boss at the gas station (which happens all the time), he will listen to them but refer them to me. Then my job is to meet with them, find out what they need, and make a recommendation to him. Relationships with staffers are just as important as relationships with Members of Congress.

If your member of Congress is opposed to your issue, you may need to reach out to other members. You want to find your best ally, not necessarily your closest ally. Issues come and go quickly on the Hill, and members rarely change a public position. In most cases, it takes a major life event to change their opinion. One example of this is Senator John McCain, who originally voted against the Affordable Care Act. When he became sick, he realized how great his health care was as a senator (and due to other factors). It became important to him to make sure others had access to the same type of health care.

Finally, don't be afraid to ask for referrals if an office is sympathetic to your issue but does not deal with it directly. All of these tips and ideas should help you prepare your issue so that it is politically grounded and relevant and targeted to the right person.

CHAPTER 3

Build Relationships, First and Always, Before You Need Them

We have been talking about building relationships and connections, and this needs to be done right at the beginning. It's possible to wait until it is too late, as in this example, where the other party literally spilled their chances into the ocean.

I'm referring to the Deepwater Horizon oil spill, a horrific event in the Gulf of Mexico, the backyard of Mississippi, Alabama, and Louisiana. We have relationships with the Coast Guard, and a couple of days after the spill we were updating the Chairman when he asked, "Well, what is BP saying?"

The room went silent, and we realized that BP had not reached out to any us. Worse, none of us had any contacts at BP either. Our boss did a press conference that day. Naturally, a reporter asked him about BP and he had to say, "My office hasn't heard anything from BP."

Within a day, BP requested a high-level meeting to reassure him that they were working tirelessly to fix the problem. Staffers have a sixth sense for when a meeting is going to be bad, and we knew this meeting was going to be bad. It's not a good sign when no one in the room can say they have a contact in a particular company.

The representatives from BP greeted us like old friends. My boss said, with all his Southern candor, "Now wait a minute; when's the last time you all have been in to visit with us or update us on what's going on with the company?" You could have bought everyone from BP in that room for a quarter, because no one could answer that question. BP not having a relationship with us was especially disturbing because they employ so many Mississippians and have a huge impact on the oil and gas industry in the state. Also, at that point, it was 2010 and my boss had been in Congress since the '90s. It was strange that he'd never heard from them at all.

The meeting was necessary from our side since we had a responsibility to everyone on the Gulf and everyone who ate food from the Gulf. But it went badly because BP had not tried to build a relationship with us until they needed something. And by then, it was too late. There were hundreds of gallons of oil pouring into the ocean. The oil spill would have made for a cold and difficult meeting in any case but, because no relationship existed, it was combative. We did not trust them and believed that they would say anything to get us off their backs at that point. It just made us push harder and fight more.

Don't wait to build a relationship. It's true that the average person will not spill millions of gallons of oil into the Gulf of Mexico. But don't chance it and wait until it's too late. Unlike BP, your ship has not yet sailed. Don't let your first meeting in an office be for a tongue lashing or the launch of an investigation. It's always tough to build a good relationship under bad circumstances.

Petitioning Is a Partnership: Make It 50/50

One of the biggest obstacles to effective petitioning is the petitioner who is demanding and insensitive and fails to make a connection. Staffers are busy. We're working on far too many issues for far too many members. This makes it crucial that your message is clear when you are petitioning.

One of the most important things I will tell you is that, when you're asking for help, you should also be offering and giving help. While staffers are busy, they still want to help you. Make it easier for them. We'll cover this issue more in future chapters where we will put together a process for preparing a "yes" proposal. This chapter will concentrate on building the relationships before you need them. The relationship is the beginning, and it is something you will have to work on continuously. You are never done building relationships.

Petitioning is a partnership, and it should be 50/50. When I tell you about relationships, many of you will think of your member of Congress. While you should have a relationship with that person, you also need to build relationships with the staffers. You are dealing with people, and you're having conversations. A conversation is a two-way street.

Many people come into the office and sound like they're reading from teleprompters. They have rehearsed to the point that they sound unnatural, making it hard for us to connect with them. Others prejudge us and think they have to talk in a certain way. For example, I've had people come in and be combative with me about issues that I actually share their opinion on.

The myth is that staffers are difficult and that you have to be aggressive to get anywhere. This is false. If you find a staffer like that, you probably shouldn't be meeting with them. Remember that the staffer would not have taken the meeting if they didn't want to help you.

I would like to give you some tips from my point of view as a staffer, based on things I've seen people do, so that you can work on relationship-building in every interaction.

First, don't feel rushed. Yes, we are busy, but we have taken time out of our schedule to help you. Rushing will not educate the staffers, and it will not help you. It's possible to rush through a meeting so quickly that no one gets anything out of it, and that just wastes everyone's time. Give yourself time to make an impact on members and staffers. The more impactful you are, the more time we will make for you.

Remember that we're farming, not hunting. You don't need to make a member or staffer your best friend or advocate at your first meeting. You're all in it for the long game. Use the first meeting to get them interested and engaged. Anything else is icing on the cake.

Don't be nervous. That's easier said than done, especially when you meet "celebrity" legislators. I've been here for ten years now, and I no longer get excited or nervous around a celebrity, but I used to. When I'm nervous, my voice quivers. For my first four years on the Hill, no Member of Congress believed anything I said because they probably thought I was two words away from tears. They would look from me to other people, as if to verify the information I was giving them. You don't want that to happen to you because of nerves. Remember that we are friendly and good at having conversations.

When you talk to a staffer, you have a captive audience because they want to help you. It's the easiest speaking engagement you will ever have. Don't be afraid to reach out. We recognize that you are human. Feel free to tell us if it's your first time on the Hill or that you are so passionate about an issue that you need to make sure you've explained it correctly. If you tell a joke and it flops, acknowledge it. Just be yourself and be honest. Many staffers are extroverts. I spend about

40% of my time writing at my desk and the other 60% talking about what I'm writing, so meetings with advocates like you remind me of why I went into public service.

We are real people, and we want to talk to and help real people. Your meeting may be a motivation for a staffer to keep doing what they are doing.

The next tip is to build the connection, not the case. You can build the foundation of a relationship in 15 minutes. You've probably met someone you liked after speaking with them for only one minute. Two minutes is enough to convince you that someone knows their stuff. Fifteen minutes is probably longer than you spend asking someone to sign your petition or getting them to register to vote. You already have experience with building relationships in a brief time.

You'll have at least 15 minutes for your meeting on the Hill. Again, we are building the connection, not the case. You don't need to secure a commitment in 15 minutes. Make a connection and use it to build a foundation.

Good relationships are not like cardio workouts. You may have heard people at the gym say, "As soon as you stop doing cardio, your heart rate goes down." And they suggest weights because the benefits last for hours after the workout. Staffers are the weights. We'll keep working for you long after you have left the Hill.

Building a relationship can also start a chain reaction. When you've established a good rapport with me, I'll talk about you to others. Not only will I refer you to, say, Congressman Kelly from Mississippi who also cares about this issue, but the next time I see his staffer I will say, "Oh, I told group X that they should stop by your office."

It's important for people to know that all of us on the Hill are interconnected. We talk about you and all the groups we meet with. We talk about the people who get it right, those who get it wrong, and those who could have gotten it right if they had a little more help.

I'll give you a few tips. First, don't use a script. You can use an outline to make sure you remember everything you want to say, but scripts just make you sound like a robot. It's hard to connect with robots. None of us, whatever our opinions on artificial intelligence, want to build a relationship with a robot.

Second, have two versions of your story: one for someone who has experienced it and another for someone who has not. This goes back to doing your homework before meeting a staffer or a member of

Congress. For example, if you're going to talk about the environment, find out, if possible, whether the person you are meeting is an avid nature lover. If they are, it will be easy for you to talk about how you want to preserve the environment for the enjoyment of future generations. If not, you'll have to find another connection.

Third, connect with them as individuals. It's important to know your audience (see Bonus Materials for staff positions and duties), but don't make assumptions based on their titles. Don't come with a negative attitude or assume they do not have enough experience or aren't trying. You may have practical experience with the issue, but don't underestimate the importance of policy experience. Do, however, feel free to ask, with an open mind, if a person has experience with your issue.

Sometimes issues fall through the cracks for myriad of reasons, but don't assume staffers are not trying.

Also, though a staffer may not have experience with your actual issue, they may have experience with your problem. If you are concerned with funding issues, you can ask the staffer to think about the last program that they worked on that was defunded. It may be a program unrelated to your issue, but the problem is the same.

And remember how closely issues are connected on the Hill. I am a Head Start preschool graduate. I didn't work on educational issues, but I meet with educators who are interested in something that falls within the national security area, for example, cyber workforce training. They talk to me about what we can do to train our workforce, starting in kindergarten. Then I can share how important early education was in my life, though it's not something that usually comes up otherwise.

Another fact about me that I often don't bring up at work is that I worked as a substitute teacher throughout law school. I taught history and math to grades K through 12. I can offer this experience to people interested in workforce training, but it will only come up if they ask me if I have experience in education or workforce training.

I just gave you a story about myself. You want to give stories along with your facts. Still on the subject of workforce training, it's not easy for us to remember the amount of money needed for the project or the number of people it will impact, but we always remember the stories. And if the stories are compelling, we will reconnect with you to get the stats. We will remember you. The goal is not to get me to memorize all your information in one meeting. The goal is to connect with me so that I can find you when I need your help.

Again, remember you need two versions of your story. If you are talking to someone who has experienced your issue, you can ask them about it—what their latest or most frustrating experience was, for example. Otherwise, make it relatable and look for a different emotional connection. Have they been similarly frustrated with a deadlock or defunding issue, for example? You might have to convince us to care about the issue. Identify why it should be important for the member of Congress and staff.

Every member of Congress gets into politics because they want to change something. No one runs for office thinking that everything is already perfect, and they just want to join the party. The desire for change is their main motivation. The same is true of staffers. Identify the change needed in your issue. Don't say, "You should be working on this." Say, "We should be changing this."

Don't just come in and demand things. Ask staffers and Members of Congress what you can do for them too - I will talk about this more in the context of coalitions. Ask what has been done before you and where the problems are. If you want to know why the health bill has been held up in Ways and Means, feel free to ask, "Is it because everyone is working on the new tax bill?" And that is not secret information, so we will tell you.

Feel free to ask us about other issues in our portfolio. There are three main reasons for us to be working on an issue, and they might affect what kind of advocate we will be: we may be passionate about the issue, it may be a "stepping stone," or it may be urgent.

If you and I are passionate about the same issue, we will work tirelessly to help you be a more effective advocate.

Don't be dismissive if you suspect a staffer is using your issue as a stepping stone. We'll be good advocates for you because we genuinely want to do well. Like anyone else, we want promotions, and for us a promotion probably means working on an issue we are passionate about. We will work hard on your issue because we want to get to our desired issue.

We see this a lot in foreign affairs. Of course, there are staffers who have wanted to work in foreign affairs ever since they did a United Nations student simulation in tenth grade. But don't be surprised to find a computer science major working on that issue. Her goal may be the cyber security portfolio, but she will be a rock star in foreign affairs in order to be first in line for the next promotion.

I wasn't an immigration and border security expert when I came to the Hill. I'd been promoted several times, but my goal was to become a subcommittee director. I wanted to be in charge of a whole subcommittee's portfolio, manage the issues, draft legislation, and figure out the hearings. To get there, I was rocking out the immigration and border security portfolio. People who met with me at that time didn't get the feeling that I didn't care about their border security issues—I did, but I also had my own goals. Don't be disappointed if you meet with someone who doesn't live and breathe your issue.

A staffer may be working on an issue because it is urgent, maybe because of a sudden international or national event. This staffer is in "crisis mode" and will be the perfect advocate for you. As in the real world, someone who helps you through a crisis will have your loyalty for life (remember that!). If you find a staffer from the Department of Defense working on your issue, a humanitarian crisis, don't assume that you won't be able to connect with them or that they will be unsympathetic to the humanitarian issues. That staffer may be a utility player and the best staffer in the office to handle crisis issues. While it is good to know a staffer's portfolio, don't get too caught up in it. Don't assume they cannot or will not handle your issue well.

Keep in mind that the staffer you were scheduled to meet may be unavailable. This happens a lot in the personal office due to scheduling conflicts and issues that "come up." Don't be disheartened or feel that you were "put off" if you have to meet with another staffer. If the staffer did not consider you to be important, they would have canceled the meeting instead of arranging for a replacement. You are allowed to be disappointed, but you have to move on.

I take meetings for my co-workers all the time, and I'm the best note-taker in the world for them. But I do more than take notes—I get all the information and tell the staffer who missed the meeting, "This group is really important, and they're passionate about this issue. You should follow-up with them." I want my co-workers to know that I do an excellent job when I take on their meetings.

And you never know why the staffer who was scheduled to meet with you scheduled me, for example, as a replacement. I might be a good utility player and can strategize with you. Or your issue may be important to the southern state delegations, and my colleague knows I have contacts in most of those offices.

How to Build and Leverage a Coalition

Next, let's address coalitions. No piece of legislation has ever become law with a single vote. Every issue needs a coalition. This section will explain how to build a coalition and keep it growing as your issue builds momentum. There are all kinds of coalitions: single-issue, temporary, and long-term. Whichever kind of coalition is right for your issue, you will need it to be successful on the Hill. We all work together on Capitol Hill, and so should you.

Coalitions can be made up of strange bedfellows. It doesn't matter who is in your coalition. What matters is that you are effective and that you keep moving and growing with the ultimate goal of a large and united coalition being to influence Congress. You're all working toward the same end goal.

Be strategic. The issue always comes first. The issue is the primary connector, concern, and driver for your coalition. We all have diverse backgrounds, but we can come together on our issues. As you plan your strategy, build a list of groups that care about your issue, regardless of their position on other issues. You can include businesses, trade associations, and individual companies and groups. Do your research and reach out to them. You want to connect with them and scope out exactly where they stand on the issue.

One example we deal with on the Hill is Walmart. At the name Walmart, some of you all smiled and some of you cringed—either you love them or you hate them, and so do members of Congress. But Walmart and other companies have been throwing money and publicity toward campaigns against human trafficking. They have been educating their employees, including their truck drivers, to watch out for human trafficking, and they penalize them for taking advantage of compromised sex workers. And they have started a national education campaign about how stopping sex work is everyone's responsibility. They work with the Department of Homeland Security on their Blue Campaign against human trafficking.

Walmart and various human rights groups work together to end human trafficking, but no one assumes all these human rights groups support Walmart's practices. They are still fighting Walmart on workers' rights, including the minimum wage, supply-chain issues, and the impact on local economies when a Walmart store opens in a community. This has not changed. But to the credit of the human rights groups, they do not allow these other issues to distract them. Walmart is part of their coalition. They can use Walmart's name and budget to advance their agenda and educate more people on human trafficking, and they can then leverage their contacts and expertise to raise awareness. This is a good example of a non-profit working with a for-profit company on a single issue.

It may surprise some people that I, a Democrat from the South, end up working with Libertarian-leaning members of Congress and their staff on warrantless searches and mass surveillance issues. But it shouldn't, because my job as a staffer is to figure out how many members and how many votes I can get to share my members' positions. Despite our differences on various other issues, Democrats and Libertarians can often work together on this national security issue.

Walmart is an example of getting a coalition right. I also want to give an example of when people get it wrong. After the shooting at the Mother Emanuel African Methodist Episcopal Church in Charleston, South Carolina, I was trying to build a coalition of groups to get a domestic terrorism bill through the House. We decided to bring together various organizations that have worked on domestic terrorism issues, along with people who have been victims of domestic terrorism.

When building a coalition, it's good to bring people from different niches together on a shared interest. That way you can build a bigger coalition. I reached out to an animal rights conservation group and an environmental safety group, each of whom I'd worked with on domestic terrorism issues before. I set up a meeting for the coalition, but the animal rights group told me they didn't want to come to a meeting with the environmental group because they were fighting over something related to the National Park Service. They wanted separate meetings.

I didn't want to minimize whatever issue they were fighting over, but I honestly didn't care because their fight wasn't related to domestic terrorism. All I cared about was getting the domestic terrorism bill through the House after the church shooting. I was annoyed and also felt that this group did not understand how coalitions work. It's not a coalition if you get distracted by other issues you don't agree on. It's a coalition when you focus on what you *do* agree on. And staffers do not want to play traffic cop. When there are urgent issues going on, you can damage relationships and your reputation if it feels like there are no adults in the room to monitor you and other advocacy groups.

Regarding coalitions and strange bedfellows, be realistic. Don't compromise yourself by working with an extreme group even if you support the same issue. There are some coalitions you should not join because you'll never recover from being associated with some of the groups in them. But you have to do your homework. You have to do a cost/benefit analysis in the same ways that we do.

Just as you should build relationships with members and staff before you need them, you should also build relationships with coalitions before you need them. You should build a coalition of members on the Hill who will help with your issues and advocacy efforts. If you ever need to move something like a bill, an issue, or a statement, you'll need a hearing. You will need Members of Congress to be a part your coalition.

We want to be your best ally on the Hill, but we cannot be your only one. You should offer to help members of Congress and their staffers to advance your calls. The way we do that is by identifying and working with other members who share our concerns. So, you want to identify your supporters, your members, and your staffers.

Don't be overwhelmed by thinking you have to create a whole coalition of 100 people and 100 members of Congress. When I say identify your supporters, members, and staff, I mean just that. Even if you only have five members of Congress in your coalition, you have to start somewhere. Tell us up front that you are building a coalition and that it's not complete. Show us your work by saying, "We've reached out to Congressman X's office, and we know that it's going through the committee with a chairman from Texas, so we are also reaching out to the Texas delegation." That way, we see that you're working.

The good news is that you are talking to staffers who strategize and build coalitions all the time. We not only know your pain, but we live it every day. So, don't be afraid to tell us, "I want to build a 100-person coalition, but right now it's just us." That's fine. We've all been there. Every coalition starts with one, and we've been on that side, too.

Here is a super tip: You should offer your coalition relationships to members of Congress and staffers. We are constantly trying to build our coalitions. If you're working on an issue and you have a coalition, or are building a coalition, you should offer to share them with us.

Say there's a bill on the Senate floor tomorrow where $10 million is being cut from the human trafficking budget—which, as an aside, is probably all of the human trafficking budget. You can offer to draft a letter in support of funding this program. Offer to send us a support letter with not only your association's name on it, but also other groups who are opposed to the cuts for human trafficking.

If the funding for the program is to be cut tomorrow, staffers are probably busy with other things: appealing to offices to vote "no," writing talking points, and answering phone calls, because everyone is calling the office to ask why the funding is being cut. Having you offer to assemble all these groups in a letter is worth its weight in gold.

Then, the member will go to the floor and state the position of your letter, how many groups signed the letter, how many people those groups represent, and how many people will be impacted. These letters are powerful, but we don't always have time to coordinate 50 people to sign one. That's where you come in, because you and your resources may be able to do so. I have a great advocate for civil rights and civil liberties who helps put together coalition letters. And if you've been working on your coalition, you already have the contact information for these people. We will talk more about support letters and advocacy asks in Part II.

CHAPTER 4

Think Like a Staffer: Build a Foundation for Your Issue

In the first chapters, I showed you how to be politically grounded and build relationships. Now I want to get into laying the groundwork for your ask, which will require you to consider your issues and your goals. This chapter will give you the footwork for the dance that will make it easy for a Member of Congress or a staffer to say yes and take action on your request.

As you read this chapter, identify the type of ask you should be making and the kind of foundation you should create for it. Remember that members and staffers, like you, do not like to fail, so make sure you're asking them for things that they can do. Create a map of small successes you and they can achieve to get to your ultimate goal.

Thinking through your issue and presentation will give you the confidence you need when talking to members. That's the key benefit of this chapter. You need to think through all the whats, ifs, and how tos, so that when you get in front of the member of Congress or a staffer, you have your footing—also known as your foundation—down.

Thinking ahead will also help you anticipate what speed bumps or roadblocks you may experience so that you are prepared for them. Some advocates who come to the Hill and present their ideas to us have not thought them through. They don't know if they need to be messaging, building publicity, or whether their advocacy ask fits into a larger legislative strategy.

Whenever we hear an "ask," we automatically start processing what's going on, such as timing. We have to think of the legislative calendar, current events, and the traditional scheduling in the House.

And we may say to the advocate, "This is what we have to consider." This makes some advocates feel like they didn't do their homework. The point of this guide is to help you do your homework, but don't worry if you find yourself in a place where you have to say, "I don't know." You can tell us something like, "I thought about the legislative calendar, but I wasn't sure if you all could get this done before the recess." As mentioned in the previous chapter on building relationships, a staffer will be happy to know that you at least considered the timing and are open to hearing an explanation about why the timing is or isn't right.

There are three facets to your issue that you should consider before you make your ask. First, decide whether your goal is messaging or movement. Second, research your issue and build a legislative history. Third, consider how the timing could advance or derail your issue. Then, I will explain the strategy of building momentum, which is sowing and fertilizing your issue in order to reap solid benefits and results.

Decide Your Focus: Messaging vs. Movement

Decide whether your goal is messaging for your issue or movement on your issue. Most people think their ask is about movement, but you need to be realistic. There is a lack of clarity on what messaging is. Let me break down and define the difference between messaging and movement for your issue, with examples.

Messaging requires you to be open and realistic about your goals. Messaging is a tool that focuses on publicity, relationships, and education. It relies on legislative history, which we will talk about in detail later, and it involves writing and public relations.

Some messaging tools are part of a continuous cycle. There are bills that are introduced in every Congress, but we know that they're not going to move. The bill will die, and we have to plan an appropriate time to reintroduce it in the next Congress. These are messaging tools that members of Congress will use for you in a continuous cycle because their views haven't changed and neither have yours. The goal isn't really to move the issue but to continue an awareness campaign around it.

For example, a Member from Texas has introduced legislation about impeaching the president. There are no signs that the bill will move, but we anticipate that the bill will be reintroduced each Congress, as long as the current President is in office. The bill has enabled this Member and others to do a lot of messaging, but they are not surprised that the bill has not actually moved in the House. It's a position statement that they can leverage.

This Member from Texas was focused on education and publicity. When your issue is aligned with a member like this, you can connect with them, volunteer, and give them other ideas about things you can do to be more helpful for your shared goals. For example, if a Member introduces an impeachment bill, it may be a great time to talk to him about getting an opinion editorial letter, or an op-ed, placed in a local or state newspaper about why the president should be impeached.

Think of some tools you can present to a member of Congress as an opportunity to use on a platform so that they can do what many of them love, which is waxing poetic on the issues they are most passionate about. Right now, not a lot of legislation is being pushed through concerning instability in Iraq. But that means it would be a great time for your Member to raise awareness about the ongoing issues and about rebuilding Iraq. It's a good time for the member to publicly lay out what he believes we should be doing versus what we are doing now.

Messaging bills have a negative connotation, but they shouldn't. We write bills, do events, and use advocacy tools all the time, and we know when something will actually move and when it's a messaging tool. We get thousands of bills referred to our committee during every Congress, and we cannot move all of them. We do outreach at members' offices to walk them through why they should introduce the bills. And staffers tell each other, "Don't worry about that bill. It's just a messaging bill." Or we'll go through what the committee can do to help message the bill without promising it will move. The idea that messaging bills are a waste of time is dated. Sometimes you need to get the information out there and raise awareness, and that's a great goal with a measurable result.

Messaging tools are effective when an important issue is being blocked or not taken seriously. They are a great way to get more people involved, push your message out to a broader audience, and to form bill coalitions.

Movement tools are the foils of messaging tools. By movement tools, I mean legislative movement, where your desired result is the creation of a change in public law, or an implementation by the executive branch.

Let's talk about what movement is and what it is not. Don't measure movement in terms of completion: the implementation of or change in a law or enforcement at the executive level. A lot of legislative movement bills and other tools are evergreen tools that you can use to continue building a foundation. We have a concept in Congress called evergreen bills, which are introduced every two years (every Congress), and everyone knows that it will take a few Congresses to get them through subcommittee. It might then take another two Congresses for the committee to consider the bill, and another Congress to get it out of committee, or through the House or Senate. Those bills are showing movement, but you'll feel like a failure if your only measurement of movement is completion. That is demoralizing to you as an advocate and to the staff who is working with you.

If you set the goalpost so far that the first down never comes, you will wear down the staffers and members of Congress who are working on your issues. Ask yourself, "What do those first downs look like?" If the bill was introduced and the committee decided to mark it up, but it failed, that's still movement. You will be able to see which members voted for the bill and committee and which members voted against it. The reasons it was opposed by some and supported by others can be added to your legislative history, and you can work backward from there.

Keep in mind that Congress is slow. The Senate is known as "the deliberate body," and the inside joke is that it's actually "the deliberately slow body." Though the House is seen as the chamber where things move fast, fast is relative. Some events and legislative calendars can speed things through, but you need to understand that this will be a slow build. Still, as long as you've thought everything through, you will continue building. It is a brick-by-brick process, and no one builds the whole foundation overnight.

Research or Build a Legislative History

Every bill needs a legislative history. When people say, "That bill came from nowhere," it's not true. And if it were, that bill would probably not go anywhere. You want to be able to describe the statutory history of a bill. A legislative history is a progress report. Progress reports are not necessarily positive or negative; they just outline the progress your issue has made through the legislative process.

A good progress report will show you whether an issue or bill has struggled to get out of committee and whether there have been contentious votes on the floor of the House or Senate. Which members have voted against it? Is there a member who has advocated for the issue, time and time again, and has built a coalition around it? A legislative history shows what Congress has done on your issue.

If the bill has never been introduced, find everything that was done short of introducing it. This goes back to the research you did in Chapter 2, searching for public statements made by members of Congress about your issue. If you're struggling to develop a legislative history using the search techniques from that chapter, look for committee hearing transcripts on congress.gov. Staffers go through these transcripts, as we need to develop legislative histories for our members' issues, and we highlight all that was said on an issue. I suggest using different colors for positive statements and negative statements. You want to know what the opposition is saying, so you can decide how to counter it.

We draft these statements into a document, and we note which member said what and the date of the hearings. We will use these documents in future work to reinforce that you have support for the issue. When multiple members share our position, we can work together to craft arguments against the opposition statements and turn those into positives.

You can also look through a section of a bill that may be important to you. Some bills require Government Accountability Office (GAO) reports. We'll talk more about those in Part II, but GAO reports are a wealth of information because they're filled with quantitative and qualitative data and statistics. GAO is the investigative group, the detectives for Congress, but they are also the scientists.

We also use press releases and statements. Later, in Part II, we'll get into how you can ask a Member of Congress to enter documents and statements into the Congressional Record. You can also pull legislative history out of the Congressional Record because members enter issues there. It's also a good place to find members of Congress who can form part of your coalition. The Congressional Record is updated daily, so it is literally a recording of all the official activities in Congress for any given day. You can go through and pull up examples of specific recordings where members have spoken about your issue and supported it or had their own press release or statements inserted into the

Congressional Record. Since these are complete documents of quotes and activity, they are a great resource. All these tips are things that people can do from the homepage of congress.gov.

Next, identify other bills and amendments related to your issue. You can do a lot of backward detective work once you know what other bills are out there related to yours, and you can connect them to your issue. Look at the referral pattern of bills—which committees the bills were referred to once they were introduced in Congress. Referral patterns are important because you can see that when some bills go to the House Armed Services Committee, they do not move as fast as bills through the Senate Armed Services Committee. So, you'll say, "Well, if this is a movement bill, then it might be better for us to go through the Senate Armed Services."

But again, if you have a messaging bill and a member House-side has one million followers on Twitter and is very engaged socially, then it might be better to ask them both to introduce the bill or work on the issue for you.

Finally, bring your legislative history to us and tell us about it. Very rarely do people come in who can talk with us about legislative history, but that's a step in our process we can never skip. When I talk to a member of Congress about a bill, they always say, "How did it get here?" and, "Did we do anything on it in the last Congress?"

When you bring the legislative history to a hearing, you don't want to overwhelm staffers. A bulleted list of the most important points is usually enough, though you will have a detailed report of several pages for your own reference. Include, for example, the fact that a similar bill was introduced in the 115th Congress or that Congresswoman Jane Doe had already included a statement in the Congressional Record on the issue. Or you can write that the GAO released a report in 2018. You just want to let staffers know that you have the information and that you have thought it through. We will follow up with you for the electronic links when we need them.

Watch Out For Timing and Events

Watch out for upcoming timing and events. On the Hill, we live and die by legislative calendars and current events, and your issue will live and die by the same timing. There are numerous reasons Congress may or may not move on an issue, but they fall into three main categories.

The first is world events, usually unplanned ones. We often think of world events as negative—terrorist attacks, mass shootings, or plane crashes—but they can be, for example, large charity events such as the Global Citizen Festival. These could be a good time for members of Congress to push environmental and human rights issues. As you consider which tools to use, think about how world events may impact your work. Think about various publicity tools, so you can co-opt what's going on in the rest of the world to raise awareness about your issue.

Another good example is the Equifax data breach. The aftermath of that event would have been a great time to talk about cyber-security, privacy, protection of personally identifiable information, data breach notification laws, etc. Asks related to these issues would be at the fore-front of everyone's mind on the Hill, and constituents would be looking to see how their legislators are advocating for them on those issues.

The next category is legislative calendars. A little background: they are created a year in advance, usually by late November or early December, and that's the legislative calendar for the next calendar year. Be aware of them when planning your strategy. You may think your issue is too important to be bound by a calendar, or that the calendar must be so full that there is no place for you. I'm not saying that Congress can only do one thing at a time. We do thousands of things at a time, but you should be realistic.

The end of the fiscal year is September 30th, so annual spending bills without extensions have to be passed by then. The level of crazy that leads up to the deadlines for spending bills is a great time for you to take advantage of the hysteria if your issues are related. If the agriculture appropriations bill is not passed by September 30, a constituents' crops will be impacted. Or the Department of Agriculture loan and insurance program employees won't be able to work, meaning loans for farmers will not be dispersed. However, if you want to come and talk about health care reform to the agriculture staffer in the middle of agriculture spending bill negotiations, your issue will fall by the wayside.

There is an easy way to find out what Congress is talking about and what issues we are working on, and we all use it: Whip calendar apps. Each party in each chamber of Congress has a whip. The whip is either the second- or third-most powerful leadership position, depending on which party is in control. Because they count the votes and make sure there are votes to pass or take down an issue before it comes to the floor.

Sign up for the House and Senate Whips' app or the Whip announcements on the party's website. You don't have to get a notification for every vote or session, but they send weekly updates of what is going on in Congress for the upcoming week. They give you a snapshot of the bills that will be on the floor and, sometimes, a summary of all that was done on the floor in the current or previous week. Use these to plan your asks.

On legislative calendars, you will see that there are periods known as recesses. I know recess conjures up images of members of Congress and staff running around outside and playing tag, but it just means a break in floor proceedings. It is important to take advantage of the recess, especially if the member of Congress is spending a couple of days in your district.

The week or two leading up to recess is a good time to pitch a district or state event for a member of Congress. Pitch big events as far in advance as possible so that members can schedule that time. We usually block out members' time in 30- to 45-minute intervals when they are in the district. (In Washington, we usually block out 20- to 30-minute intervals.) During recess, they are used to doing a lot of events with shorter planning and lead times, and they are good on their feet at these events.

So be strategic and judicious about the kind of ask that you make of a member of Congress when they are in the district. Also, keep in mind that the district staffers may be traveling and attending events with the member, so it may not a good time to request in-office meetings with them. But it may be a good opportunity to get in some substantive time with committee staffers or personal office staffers in D.C.

The third timing category involves dead zones for your issue. Dead zones are when there are no current legislative moments or events. They are like black ice. You can't see them until you hit them, and things can quickly spin out of control. They are connected to holidays and other bill issues, such as when we're talking about the Farm Bill. If a member of Congress is the chairwoman of the Agriculture Committee, and they're fighting about the Farm Bill and probably will not finish before the deadline, it is not likely that member can come to your press conference about cancer research funding. It can be detrimental for you to try to push your issue through a dead zone.

And you want to make sure staffers know that you are thinking about the long-term benefits, too. This does not mean you can't work in the dead zone; you may not be able to schedule in the dead zone. If you suspect your issue is in the dead zone but the timing is urgent, think of a way to make it relevant to whatever event is going on now by connecting the dots for staffers. For example, if you are focused on workforce training and hiring, then you may want to tie your event to Veterans Day every November. That will give the member of Congress an opportunity to come to your event or to participate in your activity and highlight the work of veterans and also the need for more jobs, workforce training, and hiring of our veterans.

If you're working on social justice issues, you can tie them to Martin Luther King Jr. Day. Get creative. If you're requesting university funding, time your request and your interactions with members of Congress around back-to-school time. Many members of Congress have children or grandchildren, and they all have constituents in school, so talking about education funding as students are returning to school is a good strategy.

Plot Your Strategy: Build a Bridge to Somewhere

Next, I want to talk about plotting your strategy. By now, you know the background of your issue, who all the players are, and what's going on. Now we will start building the ask.

Don't come to the Hill with a pie-in-the-sky request. Staffers and members of Congress do not want to disappoint you, but we're not responsible for developing your legislative agenda. As you consider your ask, remember that it is better to win at something short-term and immediate than to focus all your energy on a single long-term goal with no achievable successes along the way.

These short-term and immediate wins are still winning. A lot of members of Congress and staffers are type-A personalities, and metrics of success are very important to them. Also, as you think through giving them wins, you're also building relationships with them. If you give us big, audacious goals that we cannot reach in a reasonable amount of time, we have to keep coming back to you and saying, "We've failed." For example, if you have the bill introduced and you keep asking, "Is it allowed yet?" then we have to keep saying, "No, it's not allowed yet." And we have to go over all the things we've been doing to move the issue for you, but if you don't see these steps as wins toward the bigger goal, that makes us feel like failures. And that's going to affect our relationship.

Build a series of asks. As an example, don't ask for a bill; ask for a series of small wins. They give you momentum and a legislative history. Small asks are some of the advocacy tools that we talk about in terms of relationship building and publicity, and those tools are discussed in Part II.

A good tip is to focus on the relevance of your small wins. As you think through the process, ask yourself, "Is this issue going to build a bridge to nowhere?" You don't want a staffer or member to have to ask you why something is important or why people should care. Know the answers to these questions long before you make your ask. Remember, your issue has to connect people and causes, and it has to be transformative.

Plot your "ask" stepping stones. What can you ask for first? And if you achieve that, what can you ask for next? This is a great time to browse the advocacy asks section in Part II and think through your goals. You can work on different issues and have different goals running concurrently. Also, you must realize that some asks are universal: they may be classified as educational tools, but they also become an avenue for publicity and relationship building.

Physically chart out your end goal. On the left side of a paper, put "start." And on the right side, put "finish." Then write the ultimate goal. Fill in four or five stepping stones between the start and the finish. Staffers do this all the time, and we present it to members. The name differs between offices, but we call it The Ultimate Goal. For example, we say, "The Ultimate Goal is to keep the border wall from being built."

Then we lay out a series of Congressional hearings that we are going to put on, a series of public briefings and press conferences that we will lead, and the topics of legislation that we will introduce and how we plan to move them. We do not do this for every issue, but we do it for the big issues, as well as issues our members are passionate about. Think like a staffer and follow the same procedure.

By deciding whether your focus is messaging or movement, building a legislative history, watching for timing and events, or plotting out a step-by-step strategy, you greatly increase your chances of reaching your goal. The information in these chapters is not a suggestion to quit your day job and apply to be a Congressional staffer. But if you think like us, it will be easier for you to communicate with us, and you will have more confidence when doing so. And you will get a much better response from your efforts on the Hill.

CHAPTER 5

Building an Effective Ask

This is one of the most important chapters in this book. When I started out on this process, I learned that everyone coming to the Hill was being told, "Don't forget to make your ask." But as I sit across from people in the meetings, I often don't know what their ask is. When I leave the meetings, I still don't know what their ask is. This doesn't mean the meetings were a waste of time, but they were not as efficient and effective as they should have been.

In this chapter, I will explain the anatomy of an effective ask. To do that, we'll go through the things you should consider as you build your ask. We will make sure that your ask is targeted for the results you want, that you are using the correct tools to align your ask, and that you know how to close your ask.

Anatomy of an Effective Ask

First, I would like to break down the different parts—the anatomy—of an ask. There are five parts. By "ask," I mean both the noun and the actual conversation, the meeting that is part of the ask.

The first part of your ask is the opening, where you should acknowledge the situation the staffer or member of Congress is in. Here is where your awareness of legislative history comes in handy. Acknowledge the member's engagement in your issue to-date. If you are dealing with a new member of Congress, don't ignore what they've done with your issue before they were elected unless you're working on an education campaign that starts from zero.

Thank the member of Congress and his staff for the work they've been doing on the issue, whether it was you or another group who asked them to do it. Acknowledge how hard it is to move an issue through Congress and reiterate that you appreciate their efforts. Acknowledge the "pain points" they may have in regard to the issue: they may have had a difficult personal experience with the issue, or they may be up against frustrating barriers or strong opposition.

If relevant, acknowledge the way Member has struggled advancing the issue (again, using your knowledge of the legislative history). For example, "I know you've been hitting some congressional barriers and that this issue is one you've struggled to have considered in a mark-up," or "I know you had a press conference last year on the issue, and you have been trying to raise awareness."

You can also acknowledge the current political situation and the timing. Express your sympathy if the member is in the minority party and does not control the committee agenda or schedule. This opening serves to reinforce the relationship and also shows that you have done your homework. Staffers do this when we are negotiating oversight requests because we want other staffers to know we are engaged. This is also a way to show your expertise without showing off.

The second part is to have the right ask, a specific ask. I think some people are afraid of being specific—as if they think it will increase their odds of getting a "no." But if you don't ask for something specific, then anything can happen or worst, nothing can happen.

Let me share an example of a wrong ask. After the Las Vegas MGM concert shooting in 2017, there was a push for immediate gun control legislation. Several bills were introduced, and people also did publicity events to raise awareness of the legislation under consideration in Congress. One bill in particular caught the attention of many people outside Washington.

There are some bills that come up during every Congress, such as the Sportsmen's Act. The Congressional Sportsmen's Caucus is a group of member who care about hunting-related issues. You would think the CSC would just attract conservatives and Second Amendment advocates, but it is a diverse group of people who enjoy hunting, including my boss, one of the few Democrats in the group. His position on guns differs from those of the more conservative members, but he uses the caucus for relationship building and thought leadership.

After the shooting, people became aware that the Sportsmen's Act contained a section that would allow silencers to be purchased and used in the United States. The reasoning behind it was that the loud sound of guns discharging was detrimental to the hearing of frequent sportsmen. So, our personal office and our committee office were bombarded by gun safety and reasonable-gun-ownership groups saying that our member should not be a member of the sportsmen's caucus and asking why he was a member of the caucus.

People asked him to leave the caucus. I remember thinking they didn't understand how caucuses work. Just because he's a member of that or any caucus, it doesn't mean that he supports every piece of legislation that caucus supports. And his leaving the caucus would not get the result those advocates wanted. What they needed was for one of the few Democratic Members with authority and expertise in the sportsmen's caucus to stand up and say, "I am a part of this caucus, and I support sportsmen's rights. But I draw the line at allowing silencers to be used." These advocates were making the wrong ask.

I didn't even pass their ask along to my boss because it didn't make sense. They moved on to asking that he vote "no" on the bill. This was a second wrong ask, because he was already planning to vote "no" due to the silencer section. They also did not take into account that there were more impactful actions he could take in his position. A better ask would have been for Ranking Member Thompson to introduce an amendment to strike the silencer language and have it stripped out of the bill. Or they could have asked him to rally other reasonable gun-ownership advocates on the Hill to say they would support the bill if the silencer section were removed.

Next, make sure your ask is specific. Often, people make their asks too broad, maybe because they haven't thought through exactly what they want or what their goals are. Which is why we will walk people through that process so that, by the time you get to the meeting, you know exactly what you're asking for and exactly what goal it would achieve.

One group came in struggling with exactly what they wanted us to do. The Hill has about 20 intellectual property caucuses, and the Department of Homeland Security handles intellectual property issues concerning goods that come across the U.S. borders. But we have to be careful of what we do in the intellectual property law space as those issues are handled by the House Committee on Ways and Means and the House Judiciary Committee.

This group knew the limits of our jurisdiction, which we love. I was impressed that they not only knew of our jurisdictional challenges on intellectual property, but they were also strategic in what they knew they could ask of us. Unfortunately, though, it never translated to an ask. We had three meetings where they talked to us about the jurisdictional challenges with the other committees and about how they wanted to build a relationship with the committees so that they could work on intellectual property issues. But they never asked us to recommend to any of our members on the committee that they join their caucus.

Whether you plan to use political advocacy tools to build relationships, raise awareness, or get publicity for your issue, you do have to physically make the ask. This group is an example of what not to do. We were following along with them, and we agreed with them, but it's not my job as a staffer to say, "Do you want our members to join your caucus?" Getting members to join a caucus requires a lot of work on my part, and I'm not going to offer that to someone who does not want it badly enough to ask.

The third part of the ask is to target your result. Targeting your results means identifying the positive outcomes that you want from your ask and also the negative consequences if your ask is not implemented. It is a general consensus that it's difficult to measure your return on investment on Capitol Hill. But I believe that's because people don't know what results they want from the beginning: their true return on their investments (their time, money, and political capital).

If you want to see a return on your investment on Capitol Hill, you have to both give us the ask and tell us the tangible results that you want. You must qualify the desired results with Members of Congress or their staff. To do that, you have to check whether your asks are reasonable, as we discussed in Chapter 2. Think through where your goals fit into the legislative process as we discussed in Chapter 4.

Here's an example of qualifying your ask: Say you and your group have decided that you want a member-level briefing on an issue. Your asks are education and publicity (discussed further in Part II), and you know exactly what you want to happen at the meeting. When you have clarified that you want members of Congress on the record about their positions, you will quickly realize you don't need a briefing. You actually need a hearing because you want an official transcript for the Congressional Record.

To qualify the result, use process of elimination to find the tools that would be best used for what you want. Figure out which education and publicity tools lead you down the path of a Congressional hearing. After you use these tools, you'll see that you have laid markers or breadcrumbs down that lead to a hearing. Taking the time to qualify your ask will help you determine when and if you are successful. Knowing what you want and how you're going to get there will help you understand your advocacy return on investment.

In addition, as mentioned before, when you target your results, you are also giving us a win. Members of Congress and staffers are always trying to collect wins. As in sports, there is a half-time report every two years: elections. Every two years, members of Congress are analyzed, and the whole world learns their player stats. You hear how many bills they introduced, how many of them became law, how much money they raised, and any scandals they have been involved in. When you target your results and quantify them, it allows members of Congress and their staff to do the same, and they need to be able to collect that evidence throughout their time in service.

An insider tip: Staffers get these half-time reports every year. Like most employees at any job, staffers go through evaluations annually. We have to list the things that we've done. We do not want to turn in a list of things we're working on or that we have been working on all year. We want to show what we've completed. Much of our success on the Hill as staffers depends on the results we've gotten for you and your issues.

The fourth part is the use of tools. You want to leave tools for staffers to use on your behalf. Typically, a leave-behind is only as useful as what's on the paper. If you want to be remembered, you have to leave active tools and resources behind for us to use. Sometimes offices don't have an opportunity to follow up with you if we have questions about your data. So, give us a way to easily collect that data online whenever we need it. Understand that 80% of the research staffers do nowadays happens online. Give us resources that we can use without steep learning curves and which produce fast results.

Some of the most important tools are the leave-behinds and the one-pagers. Within the anatomy of an ask, there is also an anatomy of a good leave-behind. A good leave-behind or one-pager includes high-level talking points, important points for a member of Congress or their staff to remember, a specific ask, and relevant contact information.

A necessary caveat that people forget all the time is: Don't just leave us the contact information of people at the national level or in the D.C.

offices. Also include the local person or constituent who visited us in the office that day in addition to the Washington subject matter expert or the national office subject matter expert. Sometimes we want to follow up on the stories that the constituents have shared for a local flavor, and it gets really complicated when I have to call a middleman to follow up with the constituent.

Also, infographics are great, as well as other electronic versions and visual representations of your data. Most offices do not have graphic designers on staff, and most of us don't have graphic design backgrounds.

If you have already put your data into a great visual aid, then we'll use it, and we will use it over and over again. We have a closet full of posters, and we're hoarding them a bit, but we don't want to throw them away because we don't know when we might need to use them again. We use them at hearings, on floor speeches, and at press conferences. We just keep using them over and over again. And if that infographic is the data that your organization collected, and it's the data that you want people to see, your organization and your issue are going to get that exposure over and over again too.

If you can fit some high-level points about a constituent story on a one-pager, do that as well. Because staffers are also ghostwriters, we're always connecting statistical information to stories for our bosses. If you can give us some quick points about a story, it helps us when we have to write those talking points or that floor speech. And if your head is spinning because you wonder how you can get all this stuff on a single page, don't be afraid to play with the margins. We do it all the time. Members really like to get information on a single page. So be like a staffer and cheat the margins.

Also, we really like living documents, and we like links to current resources. The key here is helping staffers find out what they need and helping them do it fast. Don't take for granted that staffers know where all the grassroots groups are or where the subject matter experts are hanging out online. Remember, we're working vast issue portfolios, and we don't always have the most up-to-date information about where to go, because sometimes we're working on your issue nonstop for six months, and then something else happens, and we don't get back to it for three months. If people moved or if resources have changed, we don't know unless someone tells us. If you have "members-only access" locations online and if you can do it without triggering an ethics violation, give staffers access to databases or collections of information so that we can get current information without having to request permission each time.

Here are some good examples of the types of living resources you can provide. There are online catalogs of stories and stats for certain advocacy groups, such as cancer survivors or parents of children with autism. Tell us what websites have the best resources and are updated most frequently. Also, tell us what the best hashtags are to track your issues, and let us know when those hashtags change. While it's a broad example, the #MeToo movement was great for staffers working on women's rights and sexual harassment issues because that hashtag allowed them to quickly find new and updated stories to help with their policy work.

In regard to living documents, just remember that the mediums that people use off Capitol Hill can work on the Hill too. Now, of course, you have to be careful with videos. We don't always have time to get through hours-long pieces of information. But if there are snippets that explain your issue, tell us about them. Don't think that all the information you give us has to live on a sheet of paper.

The fifth part of the ask is the close. The only way to close an ask is to explain how you can help. If you don't do this, you have basically walked in, given us a ton of information, and made your requests, and then you're just going to leave. Asking how you can help is the best way to get movement started on your issue. Absolutely the best. A good relationship is two-sided and balanced.

Another thing to keep in mind is you may have had a meeting where you spoke about the opposition or barriers that your issue has been facing. And sometimes, that can come off as a bit combative even if it's unintentional. I'm not encouraging you to pretend everything is okay when it's not. Come to the Hill and talk to us about these problems. But like we say in the South, "Show up with the sugar, and keep the vinegar in your pocket." You don't want to be the person who is throwing vinegar all the time.

Whatever you plan to talk about when you come to the Hill, be nice and respectful. As an aside, 90% of the people who come to the Hill are absolutely respectful and nice, and 10% of them shoot themselves in the foot and waste their time.

Also, this is not the time to insult the member of Congress or complain about what they have or haven't done. Don't insult a different member of Congress either. You never know what the personal relationships are behind the scenes, and staffers talk to each other.

In short, the close is an opening to get the ball rolling on your ask.

A Few More Tips for an Effective Ask

As you build an effective ask, don't be afraid of the word "no." If you get a no, try to find the yes that exists within that no. Keep in mind, when staffers tell you no, it's probably not permanent or absolute. Often, if we say no, it's a timing issue or a temporary situation. No does not have to be an end. The number one thing you must do is accept the no. Don't fight it. Just note to yourself that it might mean "not right now," and not "never." Don't be afraid to find your win in that no.

Let's say that you are focused on relationship building and that you use one of the relationship-building tools. Supposed you've asked the member of Congress to do a Constituent Coffee, and the member says, "No." That doesn't mean that you haven't made steps in the relationship. You *have* made steps: You had a conversation about the Constituent Coffee. They said, "No." That's your win because you will find a way to keep the door open, just as we said about closing and asking how you can help.

If they say no to a Constituent Coffee, you can dig a little deeper and find out why. Maybe the member likes more scheduled, intimate gatherings where she knows who's coming and the topics that are going to be discussed. (You can learn more about Constituent Coffee in Part II) Constituent Coffees usually take place at a café or in an office, and the member does not know who is coming, or what topics she's going to be asked about. Some members thrive in those unscripted environments. Other members get nervous. It doesn't mean that they're not prepared. You'd be shocked at the number of members who are bookworms and research geeks. They literally just want to be able to research from beginning to end all the possible topics that could come up. And so, they won't like Constituent Coffee. Find out why they said no to the Constituent Coffee and keep the door open for a different place at a different time.

Have a Plan B. If you get a no for one thing, have a second, similar ask that you can make in that same interaction. You can also ask if you can come back at a better time to discuss a specific request. And if you're really running into a wall, ask the staff what they can do for you and allow them to offer suggestions for a better ask. Returning to my boss and the Sportsmen's Act, we could have helped those people come up with a more appropriate ask.

Another tip which is getting repetitive, but I cannot say it enough: Offer to help with any kind of administrative or specialized work. Congressional offices cannot hire you to help them, but there are ways that you can make your information and the work that you're doing helpful to your ultimate goal. Remember, congressional offices may be limited in tech staff or professional creatives, and often we get a little bit of private-sector envy. We see your beautiful maps, we see your great infographics, but we have no way to recreate them. Send us the electronic copies.

Just make sure all images, PowerPoint presentations, etc. that you send can be edited, so we can add our information to them too. One of the requirements on my committee is, if you use any numerical data, footnotes of where the data came from have to be included on the visual. But when people send us things that we cannot edit, my committee can't use your visual.

If your organization has live-streaming capabilities for unofficial activities such as press conferences or briefings, offer to live stream the event and ask us if we will retweet, or offer to tag us into the videos so that we can use that media as well. Also, some of your organizations may have awesome social media followings while some of our members of Congress do not. Offer influencers to our members of Congress to help them retweet your messages and your events. You can get more details on these offers to help in Chapter 3.

Another tip is that sometimes you need to make a "no-ask." You don't always have to ask for monumental things, and you don't have to ask for 50 small things. Sometimes you need to acknowledge that members of Congress and their staffers are already doing a lot to support you. One thing to keep in mind is, as public servants, we always know when people are angry with us, but we don't always know when people are happy with the work we're doing. It's okay to give us some feedback and appreciation. In fact, we encourage it, and we like it.

Reach out and thank us for our work. Thanking members for their work validates our efforts, and it pushes your efforts forward. For example, call us after an event. Of course you will call or send an email after we do an event that you helped us organize, but if you're following social media or watching a YouTube live stream and you see that we did another event related to your issue that your organization didn't have anything to do with, call the next day and ask to speak to the subject matter expert who worked on that issue. Then just tell them that they did a good job. You never know when that call might get you connected to the person you want to meet in two or six months when you might need to make an ask.

Another tip is to give us stories over stats. We can't remember all your statistics, but if you tell us a compelling story, a staffer will remember you, and we will contact you for the stats. Members of Congress are all good storytellers, and they love hearing these stories. They have mastered the art of telling stories, and they collect them as they go from town to town, from manufacturing plant to manufacturing plant. You want them to collect and tell your stories, so tell good ones.

At this point, we've gone over how to plan, time, and build your ask. One more important tip is to stay optimistic and confident. I think this is the most intimidating part because it's the point in the negotiation where you have to be the most vulnerable. And I know that can be scary, but you should be more afraid of what happens when you don't make a specific ask. We have talked about how busy Members of Congress and staffers are. If you put them in a place where they have to construct an ask for you, it may not be what you want, it may not produce the results that you want, or, most likely, it may just never get done.

So, don't be afraid to make the ask, don't be afraid to be specific, and don't be afraid to hear "no." Remember, we are going to give you 40 plus other things that you can ask for if you get a no the first time around.

PART II
ADVOCACY ASKS

CHAPTER 6

Making these Tools and Asks Work for You

Background

Advocacy asks require you to consider two factors: 1) where to make the requests (i.e., location); and 2) what end goals you want to achieve (i.e., purpose). Each advocacy ask is formatted for an introductory explanation.

There are three locations for you to make your advocacy asks:

Locations

- **District or State Office, known as the Home Office**
- **Member's Personal Office in Washington, D.C.**
- **Committee Office in Washington, D.C.**

Some asks can be made in two or three locations. Every congressional office and congressional committee is different. So don't limit yourself to the locations listed. If there is an advocacy ask that you want to learn more about or try, just call the congressional office and ask which office handles those requests.

Once you determine where you want to make your ask, the next step is to determine the goal of your Advocacy Ask. Goals can be broken down into three categories.

Goals

- **Education** – Advocates want to educate Congress about your issue. Maybe your issue is new or complicated, and you want to make sure Congress understands the backgrounds and issues at play.
- **Relationship-Building** – Advocates want to build a relationship with a Member of Congress. The tools are particularly helpful if

there is new Member representing you or if you have never interacted with a Member or his staffers.

- **Publicity** – Advocates want to partner with a Member of Congress to help bring awareness of your issue and to build coalitions. These tools are particularly helpful when you're past the education and relationship-building phase with a Member of Congress.

The advocacy asks are formatted the same throughout.

Format

- **Explanation** – What is this Advocacy Ask? How does it work?
- **Why It Is Helpful** – What will it do for me, the advocate, or my issue?
- **Tips** – What are some general tips I should keep in mind or know about this Advocacy Ask?

Remember from the Introduction that after you use one political advocacy tool, you may come back to the book for another one. If a tool doesn't work, again come back to the book. Take more notes. Highlight more words. As you read a passage and get an idea, write it down. It may not be a crucial tool for you right now, and maybe you can't use it today. But in six months or a year, it may be just the tool you need to jumpstart you and your issue to success.

CHAPTER 7

Petitioning the Home Office:
The Local Connection

When most people want to make a change in Congress, many think they have to take their advocacy to Capitol Hill. It can appear that all the action and work is done in Washington, D.C. but don't pass up the opportunities that are in your backyard. Every member of the House of Representatives has district offices, and every senator has state offices. We will refer to these as "home offices." In Chapter 7, we'll focus on how to petition home offices.

Slower Pace + Harder Scheduling

When Members of Congress are in Washington, D.C., they have their guard up because they are outside their most familiar and comfortable environments – their hometowns and states. In addition, their schedules are packed to capacity – sometimes they are booked solid in 15 to 30-minute increments for a full day. Moreover, they are going from meeting to meeting, group to group, vote to vote, with committee tasks in between. Members of Congress are told in one meeting to vote "yes" on an issue; then, they go to another meeting where someone says "vote no" on the same issue. Back at home, schedules are not as hectic as there are no votes or committee tasks interrupting the schedule.

Home offices often have only a few staffers and in fact, some offices have just one staffer. It's fairly easy to secure a meeting with these staffers, and sometimes they are personally close to the Member of Congress. Their positions may allow for more face-time with a Member of

Congress, too. For example, a local staffer may drive all over the state with a Senator which creates the perfect opportunity to discuss your issue if you've made a convincing case to the staffer. Also, some local staffers are close personal friends and political advisors who have worked with the Member of Congress from the beginning of their political careers.

Also, don't get hung up on the need to meet in the physical office of the member of Congress, either. A congressional visit by the Member of Congress or his staff to your place of business or volunteer event is a great opportunity for relationship-building and media exposure. Members of Congress are working in D.C. and at home, and their staffers are always looking to find activities to highlight that work. Help them highlight your needs, too!

Catching a Member of Congress in a relaxed environment is not going to be easy. You have to look at the congressional calendar to see when Congress is in session – at work in D.C. Once you view the calendar, you will see that most Members of Congress are only in their home districts and states for a weekend, or a rare full week. During that time, in addition to meeting with constituents, they have things to catch up on such as health appointments, family commitments, and a range of political obligations. Tip: Don't forget about the August recess. When Congress is in recess for 4-5 weeks, that's usually the biggest block of time for your member to be in his home offices.

Let's get into the types of Asks you can make at the Home Office.

Educational Asks

1. Informational Briefings

- **Explanation** – Briefings may be the most common way to inform Members of Congress and their staffs in a face-to-face setting. For Members of Congress, briefings provide an opportunity to learn details of a subject matter or issue directly from the experts who can offer raw data with as much detail as required. Similar benefits accrue to the staffer. Additionally, staff are more likely to develop long-term relationships with briefers. For experts or laypeople who may be camera-shy, they may be more inclined to appear at a less formal setting, such as a briefing over a congressional hearing or a press conference.
- **Why They Are Helpful** – Briefings are beneficial because the

relationships they foster can be used to facilitate the flow of information. Requests for meetings, letters, and site visits suddenly become much easier after staff have an opportunity to meet and hear from you in a briefing.

- Tips
  - » Suggest briefing topics and ideas to your Member of Congress.
  - » Be prepared to recommend briefers who can highlight your point-of-view.
  - » Help build the crowd. Members of Congress and their staff will appreciate a well-attended event. Make sure your colleagues, co-workers and friends know about the briefing. Also offer to spread the word to other Members of Congress and staff.
  - » Ask the organizing Member office if you are allowed to create a sign-in sheet. If so, use the roster of attendees to grow your own distribution lists.

2. Roundtables

- **Explanation** – Roundtables present an opportunity to have informal discussions with a Member of Congress or multiple Members of Congress in your community and Washington, D.C. The roundtable format allows you to add a number of subject matter experts from different organizations but with similar viewpoints. While these tools don't usually include formal agendas or an order of speaking, the topics are limited to a particular set of issues.
- **Why They Are Helpful** – Roundtables present an opportunity for Members of Congress to question and hear from several advocates and groups at the same time. Some Members of Congress love this informal format which allows them to be the fact-finder. These events also provide an opportunity to tell the Member of Congress and other participants about the hurdles you've run into so that they can help you strategize policy solutions or share best practices.
- Tips
  - » Most Members of Congress will be fine managing and facilitating the order and flow of the roundtable, but there should be a general discussion about order and topics.

» Because roundtables are informal, be aware of how much time you spend talking. Be courteous to others in the roundtable.

» Stay on topic. Every roundtable has specific topics to discuss. If you want to talk about an issue that is off-topic with a Member, ask for a separate follow-up.

3. District On-Site Meeting

- **Explanation** – A district on-site meeting is an opportunity for your group or company to host a Member of Congress or staff at your location or site. These on-site meetings are usually extended to large groups or groups with severe resource limitations. Having these meetings at your chosen location may provide the Member of Congress with an opportunity to visit your community or company to see where advocates live and work.
- **Why They Are Helpful** – On-site meetings help to provide color and energy for your group's issue. Think of the impact there would be if a member of Congress held a meeting in a neglected library or school that has suffered from funding cuts. Additionally, think of showing off the results of a project that was completed with help from the federal government by meeting at a new community small business accelerator.
- **Tips**
  » Resist the urge to create a false environment. Use this opportunity to provide a ground-truth setting for the member of Congress.
  » Create an agenda that includes a brief tour or showcase.
  » Know how many participants will be in the member's party, and plan accordingly.

Relationship-Building Asks

4. Constituent Coffees

- **Explanation** – Members of Congress are always looking for informal ways to connect with constituents. When Members of Congress are working in their local district offices or their D.C. offices, this presents an opportunity to have coffee with them and discuss community issues or policy concerns. Members of Congress will answer questions as asked and will also provide an update about issues being debated or considered in the House or Senate. Members of Congress are also interested in knowing what's happening in the communities they serve and not just what makes it into the local newspaper. This is your opportunity to share new information that the Member of Congress may not get from anywhere else.

- **Why They Are Helpful** – These are casual meetings to get acquainted with your Member of Congress so that you can humanize your issues, that is, put a face with a cause. You will have an opportunity to introduce yourself and ask questions or make brief comments. If you have never met your Member of Congress or it's been a while since you had some facetime with her, these coffees are a good opportunity to get on her radar.
- **Tips**
  - » Be mindful of the time you use for introductions and questions. These events are not the time for detailed discussions. Instead, they are an opportunity to lay the groundwork for a more detailed discussion later.
  - » Location Considerations: You only need a semi-quiet space that has coffee (teas, water, hot cocoa, etc.). Consider your local coffee shop or restaurant. Also, consider places where your group may organize. Think about places like the Kiwanis Club, an Elk's Lodge, American Legion Post, community library, a union hall, a school, or a church.
  - » If you organize an event, be prepared to collect and provide RSVPs for the congressional office if requested.
  - » If you organize the event, remember it is your job to promote the event with your organization and the public.
  - » Sometimes congressional offices will set up these coffees on a recurring, standing basis. Check the website first. If there is no information, just call the office where you want to have the coffee and ask.

5. Meet & Greets with Members and Staff

- **Explanation** – Meet & greets are planned or unannounced drop-by meetings with congressional offices. The meetings are usually to introduce yourself or a small number of advocates from your group. The audience for these meetings is small, 2-3 people from your organization and usually 1-2 staffers, plus the Member of Congress. These meetings are brief and are meant to talk about your group's high-level priorities or thank a Member of Congress for her work on a particular issue.

- **Why They Are Helpful** – Meet & Greets are helpful because they present opportunities to get face-time with a Member of Congress or staff without making an ask. As we discussed in Part I of the book, relationship-building extends beyond only or always showing up to make advocacy asks.
- **Tips**
  - » Scheduled meetings should be brief in nature, that is 15-20 mins. If the meeting extends beyond 20 mins, it should be at the urging of the Member of Congress or staff, not you or your group.
  - » Unscheduled meetings should be very brief drop-ins; they should be no more than 10 minutes. Many times a Member of Congress and staff will decide to take these unscheduled meetings in their office lobbies.

6. Legislative Interviews

- **Explanation** – Legislative Interviews are usually reserved for new Members of Congress. They are fact-finding and relationship-building opportunities. The interviews allow you and your group to learn and understand where a Member of Congress stands on a particular policy issue. Campaigns and election seasons don't always allow Members of Congress to address niche policy areas, so these interviews are an opportunity to explore and show your interest in a particular issue.
- **Why They Are Helpful** – These interviews give you or your group an opportunity to show a newly elected Member of Congress that you are interested and educated on a particular issue. The causal nature of the interviews also shows that you are looking to learn or understand a Member of Congress's position, rather than attacking it. These interviews are also an opportunity for Members of Congress to share their political messages and policy positions as well as increase their visibility.
- **Tips**
  - » Legislative interviews are focused on a particular set of

issues or interests, so limit your discussions to a narrow set of questions.

» Approach controversial topics politely and respectfully.

» Be prepared to follow-up after the meeting using other tools (e.g., letters, phone calls, etc.) as needed.

» You can also request that Members of Congress sit as a group for a panel legislative interview.

Public Opinion Asks

7. Meetings with Members and Staff

- **Explanation** – No single ask of a Member of Congress is more widely used than a request for a meeting. For grassroots organizers, labor unions, and corporations alike, meetings are generally secured by contacting the member's office. Most offices require meeting requests to be made in writing (i.e., e-mail). The written request should include important details such as date and time availability, a list of attendees and the purpose of the meeting. Offices usually reply in a timely manner anticipating that travel arrangements will need to be secured.

- **Why They Are Helpful** – Meetings create a platform for long-term relationship-building. They allow for face-to-face interaction and are the most direct means of influencing a Member of Congress. By placing a premium on organization, time, and personal appeal, meetings are time-tested and proven to provide effective results for advocates. Meetings also facilitate information gathering – business card collection, staff introductions, and Member reactions to ideas. No successful advocacy or education campaign ever happened without a meeting.

- **Tips**
  - » Request the meeting with as much lead time as possible.
  - » Days or weeks may pass before your request receives a final response – don't worry.
  - » Be punctual and also try to arrive a few minutes early, as members of Congress have many competing demands on their time. This is true whether the meeting is in Washington, D.C. or elsewhere.
  - » Have a plan. Designate a lead speaker. Know who will introduce the group's members, if necessary.

8. Quote Requests

- **Explanation** – Members of Congress can provide powerful testimonials and quotes about your organization's work or causes. However, many groups miss out on opportunities to collect, use, and benefit from these quotes because they forget to ask for them. Members of Congress and their staff are accustomed to providing quotes to media outlets and savvy advocates, when requested. In addition, most members of Congress are seeking opportunities to advance their position and increase their visibility on issues.
- **Why It Is Helpful** – Collecting and using quotes from member of Congress can provide infinite avenues of use. You can use the quotes in industry periodicals, organization newsletters, membership emails, or even on your grassroots website.
- **Tips**
  - » You can give examples of similar quotes your organization has used in the past to help get the creative juices flowing for the Member of Congress's office.
  - » Always get permission to use the quotes. Tell the offices exactly where the quotes will be placed and when the quotes will be used.
  - » Once the quotes go "live," follow-up with the Member of Congress's office and point of contact to provide them with the link, image, document, etc.
  - » Share any feedback you get about the quote with the Member of Congress's office.

9. Town Halls

- **Explanation** – Live Town Halls provide local opportunities for Members of Congress to connect with their local constituents, share congressional updates, and take questions from the audience. Live Town Halls can be held in libraries, churches, community centers, or other public spaces.
- **Why They Are Helpful** – Town Halls are a great way to raise awareness of your issues, and they also help you put a local face with your cause. By asking a question or speaking up at a Town Hall, you are positioning yourself to get a valuable response from a Member of Congress to help advance or reset your cause. In addition, participants of Town Halls have diverse backgrounds and your participation will be an opportunity to connect with

like-minded advocates and recruit new allies who may be attending to educate themselves.

- **Tips**
  - » Town Halls are informal, but you still need to work through what you're going to say. What stats are you sharing? Will you share a personal story?
  - » If you can, go in groups (the larger the better) to show interest. But then designate a single person to ask your questions. Everyone can stand when your group's question is being asked, but you don't want too many voices addressing the Member of Congress.
  - » Check the Member of Congress's website or ask staff if there are any upcoming Town Halls already scheduled. If there are Town Halls scheduled, attend them and participate.
  - » Spread out between Town Halls in different locations. Have different supporters attend different Town Halls and ask similar questions. The more times the question shows up on the Member of Congress's radar, the more likely you are to get a response.
  - » Staff attend Town Halls, so try to find them (we like to blend in, when we can) and get their cards before the event starts. After the event, the staffers may be rushing out with their Members of Congress for another event, so you want to connect ahead of the event.

10. Virtual Town Halls

- **Explanation** – Like Live Town Halls, Virtual Halls provide opportunities for Members of Congress to connect with their constituents, share congressional updates, and respond to questions. These events allow constituents to call in and participate via telephone or over the web.
- **Why They Are Helpful** – Similar to Live Town Halls, Virtual Town Halls help empower advocacy groups and associations by allowing personalized petitioning of Members of Congress. These events also aren't limited by legislative calendars when a Member is in D.C. or their local communities, so scheduling can be easier. Virtual Town Halls also solve the problem of geography because you don't have to be in the same place to have the event, so scheduling can be easier.

- Tips
  - » If a Member of Congress agrees to your Telephone or Web Townhall request, offer to provide the logistical setup for your group or association. Note: Some Members of Congress will use their own virtual town hall systems because they and their staff are more familiar with their own service and equipment providers.
  - » If a Member of Congress doesn't share the same position as you or your group, be aware that there is a caller screening process that happens during Virtual Town Halls. While some Members of Congress enjoy and look forward to the "hard" questions, others may screen you away.

11. District or State Press Conference

- **Explanation** – Press conferences are an opportunity to have Members of Congress speak to the press about an issue that is important to your organization. It can be an announcement of a grant award, a new manufacturing plant, or a new product invented through federal research dollars. The topic list is endless. The press conference is a great opportunity for a staged public relations event allowing the Member of Congress to present information to constituents through mass media.
- **Why It Is Helpful** – Press conference "asks" must be strategic, and there has to be a great story attached to make the event newsworthy. The story behind the press conference has to impact people in the community.
- **Tips**
  - » Locations matter. Members have a million pictures of themselves standing in front of a non-descript backdrop making speeches. Think of unique places for a Member backdrop during the press conference. Could you hold the press conference in front of a burned school that needs government funds for rebuilding? What about a seaport in front of cargo containers?
  - » Make sure there is a human interest element to the press conference. Is the announcement about bringing jobs to a community? Is it highlighting a public-interest issue like childhood education or cancer treatments?
  - » Make sure your communications team is ready to take

good photos and help with any of the audio or visual issues that may arise.

» Always, always, always send the Member's office pictures
or video of the event. If you can send them the day of,
great! If not, try not to let it take more than a day. Members
want to show that they are out and about connecting with
their constituents.

» Always tag all of the Member's social media accounts and
make sure you add her/him to all of your event social media posts.

» If the story behind the press conference impacts more
than one Member of Congress (remember you have rep-
resentation in the House and Senate) offer to do outreach
to the other offices for their participation.

12. Support Rallies

- **Explanation** – Public shows of support for a common goal have
become staples in many successful advocacy campaigns. When
a more in-your-face method is needed to take your cause to the
next level, support rallies can be the tool for you. They can take
place in Washington or locally; that choice should depend on
whether there is national interest in the issue.

- **Why They Are Helpful** – Support rallies can attract press attention and increase public awareness for your issue. Having a
Member of Congress attend/participate only heightens that attention and awareness. These rallies elevate the conversation beyond letters and into the world of traditional protests.

- **Tips**

  » Invite press. Send a media advisory to local outlets in advance and several times leading up to the event.

  » Use social media. Create a relevant hashtag to be used and
shared by those who are engaging in the topic online.

  » Have a coverage plan. Determine whether you will use social media. If traditional press outlets (e.g., local television
and newspaper) are invited or appear, have a prepared
statement or release ready to give them.

13. Radio Interviews

- **Explanation** – Radio interviews have been a staple in American political life since the days of President Franklin Roosevelt and his fireside chats. Today, advocacy groups can use them to serve an audience greater than its membership. Talk radio stations, in particular, frequently need guests to fill airtime. Encouraging your Member of Congress to speak on a topic near and dear to you and your group is ideal. As a wise woman once said, all press is good press, especially if you don't have to pay for it.

- **Why They Are Helpful** – Radio interviews are part of the public record. Any statements made on the radio can later be recalled and used to help advance the group's cause. They are a way to get a firm position statement from your Member of Congress. They are also free and convenient as they only require access to a telephone.
- **Tips**
  - » Provide talking points to the Member of Congress. This will increase the likelihood that your message goals will be met.
  - » If it's a call-in show, encourage your membership and allies to call with relevant, helpful questions.
  - » Offer feedback to the Member of Congress. This will not only let the member know you tuned in, but it will also be encouraging for them to know that you keep up with their work.

14. Podcast Interviews

- **Explanation** – Podcasts are growing as a traditionally untapped communication channel for Members of Congress. Media outlets are increasing their use of podcasts, but so are associations and activist groups. Many groups and associations have popular or self-produced podcasts for their members and allies to help them stay informed.
- **Why They Are Helpful** – These podcasts provide a great opportunity for Members of Congress to engage with industry influencers on topical and compelling issues. Because many podcasts are specifically focused, listeners and Members of Congress can dive deep on issues of shared concern and interest.
- **Tips**
  - » Treat Members of Congress like you would your other guests. Do your homework and send sample questions,

bios, and relevant podcast information in advance. It is also wise to send your audience demographics in advance of the interview.

» Remember, most Members of Congress are very charismatic, so prepare for an interesting and colorful interview.

» Many Members of Congress are thought leaders in their own right, so give them space and opportunities to talk about the future of our country, their political goals, insights, etc.

» Provide interview equipment needs and suggestions as soon as the podcasts are confirmed.

» Keep in mind that podcasts are still being introduced and growing with audiences in Congress, so your podcast may be a first for a Member of Congress and her staff. Be patient and respectful as they learn – they'll remember and be thankful forever!

CHAPTER 8

Petitioning the Personal Office

Each Member of Congress has an office and staff in Washington, D.C. serving the needs of her constituents back at home. This office is called the "personal office," and the staffers are called "personal office staff." These offices are the primary points of access for constituent visits and advocacy visits.

(Mostly) Open-Door Policy

Congressional offices will welcome you with open arms if you have a reasonable reason to be there. If you are from the home state or district, the member of Congress and staff want to leave a good impression to boost their positive image, offer good public service, and increase their odds of reelection. While not always feasible, many Members of Congress pride themselves on trying to meet every constituent who makes the trip to Washington, D.C. That becomes an almost impossible task for a large-state senator representing millions of people, but a Member of Congress's welcome mat is still going to be there in some way.

If you want to meet your Senator or Congressperson, you usually can. But frankly, a constituent who shows up unannounced and politely asks to say "hello" will often be accommodated. If you have a serious issue you want to discuss and you plan ahead, you can usually get a chance to sit down with the Member of Congress or staff and speak directly about the issues that impact you. In short, you can directly advocate in front of the decisionmakers.

The down side of the open-door access is that you are only one of many voices. Personal offices have a handful of staffers who are in charge of legislative issues. Generally, the Legislative Director is in charge of all policy issues, the Legislative Assistant is the point person on a specific issue, and Legislative Correspondents help out with responding to letters (see Bonus Materials for staff positions and duties). Most meetings in a personal office consist of sitting down and discussing your issue with a Legislative Assistant for somewhere around fifteen minutes to half an hour. More senior staff or the Member of Congress may visit with you briefly too.

The following are advocacy asks you can make to personal offices.

Educational Asks

15. Industry Days

- **Explanation** – Industry Days are a good way for members of Congress to connect small business communities to federal agencies to promote contracting opportunities. Federal agencies set small business contracting and procurement goals, and Industry Days allow both stakeholders to connect. Federal agencies and their contracting officials will present information about future programs, initiatives, and requirements for contract bidding. These events are also great networking and educational opportunities for small businesses looking to contract with the federal government. Members of Congress, especially committee chairs and ranking members, can request to co-host Industry Days in Districts/States or at other events. Members of Congress can also request that their home districts/states be considered for future event locations.
- **Why They Are Helpful** – Industry days are a very valuable resource for businesses that work with the government. They allow you to gain the insight you need into marketing your product to government agencies, and they give you the opportunity to make necessary connections and to network with the appropriate agency.
- **Tips**
  - » Make sure to target industry days effectively. If you are a small business, be sure that the one you are attending targets small businesses.
  - » Research the agency before the event.
  - » Review the agenda before you arrive.

> » Use any break time to network.
> » Be prepared to actively participate.

16. Dear Colleague Letters

- **Explanation** – Dear Colleague letters are letters from Members of Congress to other Members, which are widely distributed to congressional offices. Staffers send Dear Colleague letters on behalf of Members and committees to request cosponsors, legislation supporters, or in opposition of legislation. Staffers can also collect signatures, request event RSVPs, and update congressional offices on administrative rules.
- **Why They Are Helpful** – Dear Colleague letters can be helpful to raise awareness of your issues with other congressional staffers and Members of Congress. You can request that a Member's office send a Dear Colleague letter to help ensure staff attendance at your organization's policy briefing. You can also ask that a Dear Colleague letter be sent around to help raise awareness for a bill your organization is supporting or opposing.
- **Tips**
  - » These letters are named after their opening greeting, which is "Dear Colleague." Staffers refer to them as "DCs" too.
  - » Staffers subscribe to Dear Colleague letters based on their subject matter expertise, so think through the broad categories your DC letter might fall under.
  - » There are hundreds of Dear Colleagues circulate each week, so you're going to have to send them
  - » Understand that many staffers have separate inboxes and ways to manage the massive amount of Dear Colleague letters we receive each day. If you want to ensure a particular staffer receives your Dear Colleague, you may want to "flag" it for them in a personalized email.

17. Member Letter to Agency

- **Explanation** – You can ask your Member of Congress to send a letter to a specific agency on your behalf based on your organization's needs. Each federal agency has a specific purpose such as national security or finance. If your organization has needs related to one of these agencies, then you can request that your Member of Congress send them a letter.

- **Why Is It Helpful** – Using your Member of Congress as a link to federal agencies allows you to make effective contact with federal agencies. Your Member of Congress has authority with these agencies, and if they make a request on your behalf, this makes it more likely that they will meet your organization's needs. While you can contact agencies yourself, going through your Member of Congress is a way to make sure that the agency's response is timely and complete.
- **Tips**
  - » Draft the letter for your Member of Congress, including all important elements.
  - » Convince your Member of Congress why your organization or cause could benefit from the specific action of an agency.
  - » Be sure to include specific details, anecdotes, and data to back up your request.
  - » Request specific action from both your Member of Congress and the agency. Make sure your Member of Congress knows exactly what you are asking for.
  - » Send your Member of Congress a thank you letter afterwards.

18. Congressional Record Statement

- **Explanation** – The Congressional Record is published every day that Congress is in session. Often, these statements encompass various events or issues from each congressional district. There are four main sections: The Daily Digest, House Section, Senate Section, and the Extension of Remarks. Your statement will be included in the "Extension" section, which is the section where your Member of Congress can insert any phrase he or she deems relevant.
- **Why It Is Helpful** – Everything in the Congressional Record is public record, which means that your statement will be accessible to anyone who searches the Congressional Record archives. It informs the public about your organization's goals, mission, or accomplishments.
- **Tips**
  - » To find previous statements from your city, you can search the Congressional Record by typing "city of (your city)."

This will give you examples of what has been requested in the past. You can use some of these as templates to build your own statement.

» It helps to draft a statement before approaching your representative.

» Not all congressional offices choose to submit remarks.

19. Member Championing – Be A Leader

- **Explanation** – As a constituent, you have the right to ask your member of Congress to champion the issues that are important to you and your community. You can ask your member, through various means, to prioritize a specific issue and to emphasize it in their platform. Members of Congress typically choose a few important issues on which they want to take the lead and champion. It's important for their constituents to make sure that those are issues that are significant within their community and that they are fully informed about them.

- **Why It Is Helpful** – If you can convince your member to champion your issues, it will be far easier to introduce legislation. In addition, they will focus on those issues when they talk with the media which results in increased national awareness. If a Member of Congress champions your issues and asks others to do the same, the better your chance of changing policy.

- **Tips**
  » Be sure to build momentum around the issue in your community in order to build awareness.
  » When given the chance, demonstrate to the member of Congress why and how your issue impacts the constituents.
  » If your Member of Congress mentions or takes action in a positive direction surrounding the issue you want him or her to champion, then you can write a letter to the editor commending this.

Relationship-Building Asks

20. Receptions

- **Explanation** – Hosting a reception for your Members of Congress can offer participants the opportunity to participate in advocacy, as more people can attend than a typical congressional meeting. In addition, you can invite the Member of Congress to serve as a keynote speaker or as a participant on a panel.

- **Why It Is Helpful** – A reception shows that there is support for your organization's cause based on others present at the reception. It also allows you to thank your Member of Congress for any past action that he or she has taken on behalf of your mission.
- **Tips**
    - » Be sure to indicate the role that your Member of Congress will play. Will he or she be a guest? A speaker? Do you want him or her to serve on a panel? No matter the role, make sure that the responsibilities are clearly articulated.
    - » Talk about why it will benefit your Member of Congress to attend your reception. For example, "Because you are committed to (issue), we believe that this will be an excellent way for you to (learn about/speak about/etc.) (issue).
    - » Be clear about the focus of the reception.
    - » The more people present, the better. If you're from a small state that isn't close to D.C., this can be more difficult. But in this case, smaller numbers can still be effective.
    - » Make sure to check the member of Congress's availability before scheduling a date.
    - » For a catered reception, you will likely need to go through the Senate and House caterer.

21. Group Photos

- **Explanation** – Taking a group photo with your Member of Congress after a meeting or gathering with them is a way to solidify your relationship, demonstrate your mutual support, and to boost publicity for your cause.
- **Why It Is Helpful** – Taking a photo with your Member of Congress is an excellent way to memorialize the event or gathering in which they took part. It offers evidence of their support and helps to hold them accountable. It also gives your organization and the Member of Congress mutual publicity.
- **Tips**
    - » Share the photo on social media for optimal visibility. Be sure to tag the Member of Congress who is in the group photo and all other members to increase the scope of the photo's audience.

» Caption the photo and be sure to include information about your group's goals and reasons for meeting with the Member of Congress.

» Offer links or further information about how people can get involved or further contribute.

Public Opinion Asks

22. One-minute Floor Speeches

- **Explanation** – A one-minute speech is a very short speech that is made by Members of Congress each business day. The speeches themselves cannot exceed more than 300 words; however, anything longer will be included in written form in the Special Orders of the Congressional Record. The Speaker of the House can grant recognition for the speech. On some days, the speeches may be limited to a set number, and on others they may be unlimited. After one minute, the person speaking can only finish the sentence but cannot add any more content. The leadership "theme team" of each side generally chooses to focus on a particular topic, but the speeches are not always limited to these topics. Participants usually sit in designated seating areas and receive priority recognition. If the business of the house is particularly heavy, then these speeches will be made at the end of the day rather than at the beginning, but only if the business does not go past midnight.

- **Why It Is Helpful** – Through a one-minute speech, you can inform other Members of Congress and their staff about your organization and your cause. Because it is entered into the Congressional Record, the statement will be public record and can be seen and searched by anyone who wishes to find it.

- **Tips**

  » The Member of Congress does not need to reserve the time to deliver a one-minute speech in advance; however, the leadership of the member's respective party may decide to organize so that the speech is delivered based on the party's message on a particular day.

  » Don't panic if the entire speech cannot be finished in one minute. The rest of it can be included in writing in the Congressional Record.

23. Industry Conference

- **Explanation** – If you are holding an industry conference, you can invite your Member of Congress to be a keynote speaker or a panelist. If an event is considered a "widely attended gathering," then the Member of Congress may make an appearance and potentially participate in the event. "Widely attended" means that there must be at least 25 non-congressional attendees. Upon inviting the Member of Congress, the event must be approved as being considered "ethical."

- **Why It Is Helpful** – When you invite your Member of Congress to speak at your industry conference, you are making a beneficial connection and making sure that your member of Congress understands your industry's needs. He or she takes on an active role in your community and in your industry. There may be a chance for them to answer questions and to discuss the industry's relationship to the government. It is a chance to make sure your industry's needs are represented.

- **Tips**
  - » It's a good idea to first call the office and ask how they would like to receive the formal invitation.
  - » Do your best to keep the invitation to one page.
  - » Put the invitation on official letterhead.
  - » Try to make sure that the letter goes directly to the Member of Congress's scheduler.
  - » After sending the invitation, be sure to follow up.
  - » Confirm all key details with the scheduler or Member of Congress.
  - » If media will be in attendance, ask if you should coordinate with a press secretary.

24. Press Backgrounders

- **Explanation** – A press backgrounder is usually one part of a media kit that includes press releases or advisories and is meant to inform the media about a particular issue. It usually provides important background information without requiring you to add too much content to the other parts of your media kit, such as the press release.

- **Why Is It Helpful** – A backgrounder is an important component to your media plan. It allows journalists and media outlets to fully understand your ideas and organization so that they can more clearly write about or understand what your organization is doing. It's a useful tool for every organization to take advantage of. Building public support for your cause through the media can allow you to influence your Member of Congress.

- Tips
  - » In your backgrounder, detail your organization's history, your mission, how your organization started and who started it, and any other details you might deem pertinent.
  - » You can include a backgrounder anytime a journalist is writing a story about your organization or an event you are holding in order to make their vision more complete.

25. Trade Opinion Editorial, a.k.a. Op-Ed

- **Explanation** – Requesting that a Member of Congress write an op-ed for your organization's specific trade publication is a way to show your organization's members that Congress is engaged and interested in your issue. It's also a great way to reach new readers and encourage advocacy for your policy goals. More, op-eds inform and engage the public and can be used as a way to sway public opinion.
- **Why It Is Helpful** – An op-ed is a great way to inform readers about your mission, organization, and issues that are important to your group and to the community.
- **Tips**
  - » The member's letter will attract more attention. And, if the issue is gaining attention, then more people will read it and find it relevant.
  - » Make sure the member understands your organization's position on the issue.
  - » Offer to help staff with any technical questions or background as they assist with writing the op-ed.

26. Referral Meetings

- **Explanation** – You can request that your Member of Congress help you gain access to another Member of Congress with whom you need to engage for your organization or issue. Often, it is difficult to gain access to a member if you are not among their constituents. Members of Congress are first expected to represent their constituents, so they are less likely to meet with someone who they do not represent. However, they will be likely to respect the opinion of another Member of Congress.

- **Why Is It Helpful** – You can use your own Member of Congress to request a meeting with another Member when that Member of Congress is more likely to make decisions or implement policies that impact your organization or issue. In addition, you can request that the staff of your own Member of Congress get in contact with the staff of another Member of Congress. Even if you can't meet with the member directly, their staff may hold persuasive power. This is beneficial because you may work in an industry or with an organization that your Member of Congress rarely interacts with. When this occurs, you can still ask your Member of Congress if you can meet with another who may hold more power over your industry or organization.

- **Tips**
  - » Discuss why it is necessary to meet with another Member of Congress.
  - » Know specifically what issue or piece of legislation you wish to discuss.
  - » Request specific action from the Member of Congress with whom you wish to meet.
  - » Follow up with both your Member of Congress and the Member of Congress (or staff) that you met with.

27. Appropriation Committee Request Letter

- **Explanation** – A request letter to the appropriations committee is a way to ask them to prioritize certain programs for that fiscal year. This gives you the opportunity to assess and address needs. You can write to your member of Congress to encourage them to write the letter to the appropriation committee.

- **Why It Is Helpful** – This is a way to gain much-needed funding for your organization. Requesting that your Member of Congress include your organization in an appropriations letter to ask for the funding that you need will allow you to function more fully and to serve more people. It can allow you and your organization to better serve your community.

- Tips
  - » Describe why your program is important.
  - » Include examples about how your organization has impacted the community.
  - » Talk about how you need a certain amount of funding for your organization to properly operate.
  - » Discuss specific numbers. If you do not receive X amount of funding, that is X amount of people who your organization cannot reach, serve, etc.
  - » The specific amount that you are requesting
  - » The amount that was included in the prior FY

28. Social Media Tags and Hashtags

- **Explanation** – Social tagging is an increasingly useful form of metadata that allows you to build relationships with others who are interested in, or are searching for, the tags that you used. You can use tags to identify the kind of resource you are providing or to situate yourself as a legitimate source. If you tag a specific person in a post, then they are more likely to see it and to give your issue attention. In addition, their followers or audience are more likely to see what you are trying to share. A social tag is, essentially, a way to increase visibility.
- **Why Is It Helpful** – Using the appropriate tags can better guarantee that your posts or other forms of online media can be seen by those who would be interested. They in turn might share the post, picture, etc. and increase your organization's exposure. This is a great way to increase public support and to increase the circulation of your ideas or knowledge about an issue.
- Tips
  - » Learn about metadata and how it can benefit your organization.
  - » Most engagement happens within the first few hours of posting content, so be strategic about your timing.
  - » Make sure that all settings for your social media accounts are set to "public."
  - » Take pictures and make videos during all of your events and then tag the issue, the event, and your lawmakers.
  - » Encourage anyone attending your events to use relevant tags to increase circulation.

29. Member Updates to Constituents

- **Explanation** – You have the right to ask your Member of Congress to keep you updated on any information that may be relevant to your issue or cause. This can include grants or internships, for example. You can also request that your Member include any information about your issue or organization in a newsletter that they send out.
- **Why It Is Helpful** – You can use your Member of Congress as a source of information to build financing and support for your issue or organization. For example, if there is a grant that could provide funding for your organization, you can find information about this through your Member of Congress. In addition, you can further garner constituent support in your community through using your Member to distribute information.
- **Tips**
    - » Call or email your Member of Congress in order to ask that you stay informed on specific issues.
    - » Include information about your cause and let the Member or staff know what information you need and why.
    - » When requesting to have information put into a newsletter, it helps to find out who is behind its creation and distribution, and to ask to speak to them (if not the Member) directly.

30. Congressional Caucus

- **Explanation** – A congressional caucus is when different Members of Congress meet to discuss and pursue their objectives. Caucuses are formed based on one mission, goal, or theme. Typically, a member of Congress joins a caucus to bring attention to a specific issue. Usually, this issue is one that greatly impacts their community or to which they feel personally connected. Caucuses can be partisan or bipartisan, and there are caucuses on a number of different issues. The goal is to raise awareness and to pursue federal policy changes or implementations that will help those they represent. Members need to attend briefings, receive email updates, raise awareness of their issues, attend events surrounding their particular issues, and network with other interested parties.
- **Why They Are Helpful** – Congressional caucuses can act as an important link between activist organizations and the federal

government. Your organization can work directly with a congressional caucus to integrate, and collaborate on, your ideas. You can also encourage your Member of Congress to join a caucus by demonstrating that a specific issue is of particular importance to your community.

- **Tips**
  - » If you are encouraging your Member of Congress to join a caucus, then you should write them a letter stating why it is beneficial for their constituents to be a part of that specific caucus.
  - » If your Member is already a part of a caucus you value, you can write them a thank you letter.
  - » Sign up for the caucus newsletter or press alerts.

CHAPTER 9

Petitioning a Committee

Committees are incredibly powerful and can often take significant actions on policy issues within their scope of expertise or authority. Because congressional committees can authorize or appropriate spending for government agencies and then investigate how those agencies are doing, agencies listen to their committees of jurisdiction.

One of the primary functions of congressional committees is to review, draft, and change bills/legislation. Every congressional session (two calendar years), thousands of bills are introduced by Member of Congress. However, only a small of number of bills become law. For example, in the 115th Congress (2017 and 2018), 13,556 bills were introduced in Congress. Only 443 of them were signed into law. Committees also have a wide range of power to investigate the executive branch, private companies, organizations, and individuals to help carry out their legislative functions, such as passing laws and monitoring the executive branch.

Specialized Advocacy

Most of the serious and specialized legislative work is done by congressional committees. Congressional committees and their staff have expertise on the issues within their scope. A committee's scope of expertise is known as a committee's authority or jurisdiction (See Bonus Materials for a classification of committee authorities and jurisdictions).

A Congressional Committee is controlled by its Chairperson, who is a senior Member of the majority party in charge. The most senior

Member of the minority party on a committee is called the Ranking Member. The Chair can unilaterally call for public hearings and can influence the development of any legislation in the Committee's authority or jurisdiction. The Chair also has almost complete control over reports that go along with passed bills, and those Committee Reports are often viewed similarly to laws.

This may be a bit of a stereotype, but by and large committee staff keeps exclusive company, and many advocates are afraid to reach out to committee staff. While it is true that committee staff do not represent individual constituents, it is important to remember that they represent every constituent.

Committee staff meetings are focused on specific policy areas with stakeholders from U.S government, international public officials, and the private sector. In order to get in front of committees, you need to focus on the authority or jurisdiction of the committee. You must pitch the importance of your issue to key priorities and initiatives underway at the committee.

Below are advocacy asks you can make of committees.

Educational Asks

31. Congressional Hearing

- **Explanation** – Congressional hearings are held by congressional committees to gather information and opinions about proposed legislation or current laws, conduct investigations, or oversee and evaluate federal agencies and programs. These hearings are usually open to the public and can be held on Capitol Hill or elsewhere. Note: more information about hearings is provided in Chapter 9.
- **Why It Is Helpful** – The opportunity to have your questions asked by a Member of Congress allows the public to associate your questions and concerns with a member. These questions and the responses will then become part of the official hearing record. From there, you can follow up with a member's office or the committee to plan next steps.
- **Tips**
    - » All congressional hearings are streamed live. You can visit the committee's website to view previous hearings.
    - » Public hearing transcripts are available at congress.gov.

32. Minority Forums

- **Explanation** – A minority forum is a way to provide a space and a platform to discuss issues that are relevant to the minority party. Similar to committee hearings, minority forums usually focus on one issue. Minority forums can be structured in a number of different ways. For example, they can be structured as a panel discussion or with designated witnesses who provide testimony. Members of a congressional committee can attend the forum and ask questions to help with their congressional duties.
- **Why It Is Helpful** – Minority forums allow a platform to discuss issues that are important to the minority party. Your group can use minority forums to highlight issues that may not be addressed by the majority party in charge.
- **Tips**
  - » If a member agrees to host a minority forum, offer good speakers or experts on the issues to sit on the panel.
  - » Make sure to include speakers with different backgrounds in order to allow for multiple perspectives on an issue.
  - » Offer to help invite and alert the media. Also offer to help spread the word about the forum on social media platforms.
  - » Minority forums are tough to organize, so be sure to thank anyone who participates, especially the members who attend.

33. Committee Correspondence (Letters)

- **Explanation** – You can encourage your Member of Congress to reach out to a specific committee if it is relevant to your cause or to your organization. If requested, your Member of Congress can send letters or inquiry on your behalf. In addition, if there is a committee whose support you would like for a piece of legislation, you can request that your Member of Congress write a letter asking that they consider it.
- **Why It Is Helpful** – This means that even if your member of Congress doesn't sit on the relevant committee, you can still request contact with that committee. This is particularly important if the committee works closely on an issue your organization is involved with. Your member of Congress can help convince the committee to further investigate an issue or to work on passing legislation surrounding it.

- Tips
  - » The most important part of this process is convincing your Member of Congress that your issue is worth communicating to a committee.
  - » To do this, it may be necessary to set up a meeting with your Member of Congress.
  - » Present your Member of Congress with all details necessary to convey the importance of the issue. In addition, you should tell them specifically what it is that you want from committee contact and how you want them to proceed.

34. Congressional Delegation (CoDel) Travel

- **Explanation** – Congressional delegations (CoDel) sometimes take official visits beyond Capitol Hill to U.S. and international locations. The purpose of these trips is generally to collect information, interact with communities, or to build solidarity with another country. The issues have regional or global significance and cover a wide range of policy areas. Usually members of Congress go with a specific purpose in mind, and the CoDel can be restricted to one geographic location or country or may be spread throughout many. CoDels, when they go as planned, are good ways to build diplomacy outside of Washington, D.C.
- **Why Is It Helpful** – These trips can influence legislative policy. Although they have been called a joke and viewed as a waste of funds, these trips help members understand the state of affairs in other states or nations. If your particular organization or advocacy-based goals involve a specific location or international trade or relations, then discussing this with your member of Congress or encouraging him or her to travel is a good way to leverage these trips. After CoDels end, you can also ask what members learned to help build expertise and relationships.
- Tips
  - » Travel opportunities allow you the opportunity to engage with your member of Congress on relevant issues abroad. You can reach out to the member and their staff to make sure that they have the necessary background information on the issue at hand.

» You have the opportunity to recommend travel itineraries and to recommend meetings that your member of Congress should set up.

» Reach out to your member of Congress well in advance of the trip to be sure that staff have time to solidify the travel itinerary.

» Try to set up a meeting in order to brief Members of Congress about anyone you would like them to meet with.

35. Freedom of Information Act (FOIA) Request Help

• **Explanation** – Under the Freedom of Information Act (FOIA), you can request information that falls within certain categories from the executive branch. This includes various records and other information that is made accessible to any person who makes a request. FOIA requests exist to keep the executive branch of government in check.

• Sometimes, however, your FOIA request will be delayed or fail. Members of Congress have the responsibility to perform oversight investigations of the executive branch in order to request and withdraw information necessary for the American public. If an oversight issue is important to you and your community or district, then you can request that a congressional committee perform an oversight investigation outside of your FOIA request to the executive branch.

• **Why It Is Helpful** – You have the right to access certain information and to hold your government accountable for that information. You can request documents through FOIA, but if the FOIA failed, you have a right to appeal that decision and to work with your congressional committees to keep information transparent and to hold the executive branch of government accountable.

• **Tips**
» When submitting a FOIA, you should know that you do not submit the request to one central government database. There are 430 Federal agencies, so the process can be somewhat complicated.

» For the FOIA request, the agency is required to respond within 20 business days.

» The authority of Congress to launch an oversight investigation comes from their constitutional "implied powers." These powers are almost always carried out by congressional committees.

36. Notice of Proposed Rulemaking (NPR) Comments

- **Explanation** – You have the opportunity to write comments on proposed regulations through what is known as "notice and comment." The courts have the ability to deny a regulation if the responsible department cannot legitimize or explain the reasoning behind the regulation. A regulation is legally binding; however, during the "notice and comment" period, individuals can put their input in writing. Then, when issuing final regulations, the department in question must respond to the comments. The department will issue a "Notice of Proposed Rulemaking" followed by the comment period. After comments have been issued, there is the issuance of the final rule, after which the 30-day delay goes into place before the regulation is established.
- **Why It Is Helpful** – The comments placed within the "notice and comment" period will determine what regulations are or are not passed. Everyone can post their comments through regulations.gov. Although departments tend to favor well-known and well-funded organizations, writing a well-thought-out response can get your desired agency's attention and ultimately sway the decision-making process. Submitting your comment to your Member of Congress can allow them to know your stance, and you can also encourage them to submit their own comments. If your comment can demonstrate that there are problems with the proposal, then the regulation may not be passed.
- **Tips**
    - » Using data will make the department privilege your comments. While narrative can be used, it can be optimized with the use of quantifiable information.
    - » Be sure to support your comment with legal and policy-based information to demonstrate why a regulation should not pass or be enacted into law.
    - » Make sure that your comment is well-organized and easy to read. This means organizing your information accordingly, and also appropriately referring to specific parts of

the regulation, complete with page numbers and paragraph when using quotations.

» You can also recommend alternative regulations. If a regulation is trying to meet an objective, you can explain how the same objective can be achieved through a different route.

37. Bill Report Language

- **Explanation** – The report language of a bill is the content of the committee report that accompanies that bill and any additional explanatory statements that are required. The committees are required to write a report that will be attached to the bill and an accompanying statement of explanation. These reports typically include the expectations of the bill and any spending restrictions for the specified activity or project. They also include congressional intent. It is possible for you to speak with your Member of Congress about the included bill report language.
- **Why Is It Helpful** – This is where your Member of Congress justifies the budget request. It helps to determine the purposes for which federal dollars can be spent and how much can be spent. It's useful to know how you can convince your Member of Congress to encourage the authorization and appropriation of spending on particular programs or issues. External factors are largely considered when determining the course of the appropriations process. These external factors may include the interests of outside groups who can communicate and submit their own report language. As a result, you can be influential in the formation of the report language.
- **Tips**
    - » Write a letter to the appropriations committee clearly articulating why they should invest in a specific program.
    - » If you can, set up a face-to-face meeting which will allow you to situate yourself as an expert and convey the importance of your program.
    - » Organizing a site visit can show firsthand how your program benefits the community and can result in increased funding.
    - » Use specific anecdotes and numbers to show how your organization has impacted those it is designed to serve.

38. Questions for the Record (QFRs)

- **Explanation** – Questions for the Record are designed to hear follow-up questions; think of them as take-home exam questions. The written questions are sent to committee hearing witnesses after they testify before Congress. Witnesses must respond to the questions in writing, and the questions and responses become a part of the Congressional Record.
- **Why They Are Helpful** – Advocates can send questions to staffers to be included in the QFRs which were not asked or clearly answered in the hearing. This is a good place to ask for statistical or financial data that would have been difficult for a witness to articulate or explain during the hearing. You can also ask questions that relate to historical information which may have predated his/her arrival at a company or department. Hearing witnesses are frequently high-level officials or company executives, so sometimes the questions are too technical for immediate answers at a hearing. QFRs allow for the questions to be sent to experts within the agency or company who have a greater knowledge or understanding of the issue at-hand.
- **Tips**
  - » The morning after the hearing, email the potential questions to the subject matter experts on the committee's staff or in a committee member's personal office and ask if you can give them a call in order to discuss the QFRs.
  - » Don't send more than 2-3 potential questions, unless more are requested by staff.
  - » QFRs are usually required to be submitted by staff within 7-10 days of the hearing.
  - » Set a reminder for the witness response deadlines to follow-up with staffers.
  - » Note: Executive agencies and departments are notorious for missing QFR deadlines. Don't bug the staff; there is very little they can do to force a speedy response.
  - » QFRs can also be pronounced as "Q-fors."

Relationship-Building Asks

39. Site Visits

- **Explanation** – It is not uncommon for Members of Congress

106

and their staff to visit sites to determine how a company or organization is serving or employing a community. Visiting these places firsthand allows them to interact with constituents in a more meaningful way. It also impacts the way they will vote when it comes to certain initiatives. For them, site visits can help to build voter support and to determine what issues require more attention.

- **Why They Are Helpful** – Site visits are helpful ways to educate your Member of Congress in person about a specific issue and about your organization. You can build a relationship with your Member of Congress firsthand and position yourself and your organization as an available expert. In addition, you can prove the relevance of your organization by demonstrating that you are making a difference in the community your member of Congress represents, which just so happens to be the community where you live.
- **Tips**
  - » Organize your site visit during a recess when a member of Congress returns to your city or town.
  - » Be punctual and professional.
  - » Be patient with your member of Congress if she needs to interrupt the meeting due to competing congressional commitments.
  - » The time for the visit may be limited, so be sure to underscore the most important parts of your organization.
  - » Have live demonstrations available to show the member of Congress.
  - » Be sure that everyone involved knows what to do, like who's speaking and who's demonstrating different activities.
  - » Conclude by giving the Member of Congress specific ways they can take action to help your organization.
  - » Be prepared to answer questions from the member of Congress and staff.

40. Cold-Calling To Speak with a Subject Matter Expert (SME)
- **Explanation** – This is a tactic that you should use sparingly. Cold-calling a staff subject matter expert (SME) is essentially a way to make sure that you have a point of contact with whom you will follow-up with via email. While you will not ask them any

questions on the phone, you'll use this quick connection tool to establish who it is that you will be talking to in a Member's office and to make sure that you will send your emails to the correct point of contact.

- **Why Is It Helpful** – Cold calling a SME is a way to make sure that you have the correct contact information before sending emails. This also serves as a way to let the SME know that you will be following up with emails or a series of emails. Sometimes, this advocacy tool is preferred by some offices rather than email blasting hundreds or thousands of staffers at once.
- **Tips**
  - » Keep your call brief. Remember you don't have an appointment with this staffer. It shouldn't last more than a minute, unless the staffer pushes for more information from you.
  - » The only information that you need to include is a brief background about your organization and a confirmation that you have the correct email.
  - » Don't be offended if the office gatekeeper doesn't allow access to the SME; remember you don't have an appointment.

Public Opinion Asks

41. Hearing Questions

- **Explanation** – Congressional hearings are ways in which the congressional committees analyze information, investigate organizations and companies, and conduct oversight over agencies. While the nature of hearings varies, they all carry a somewhat similar procedural format. Most hearings are open to the public; however, the committee can choose to close a hearing based on certain rules. In advance of hearings, the public can submit questions to be asked of witnesses.
- **Why It Is Helpful** – The opportunity to have your questions asked by a Member of Congress allows the public to associate your questions and concerns with a member. These questions and the responses become part of the official hearing record. From there, you can follow up with a member's office to plan next steps.
- **Tips**
  - » While these hearings are public, there may be limited space to attend in-person.

» All congressional hearings, even field hearings held outside of Washington, D.C., are streamed live. Just visit the
committee's official website to see if your question was
asked.

» If you miss the live streaming, most congressional committees have YouTube channels which include recordings
of previous hearings.

42. Committee Statements for the Hearing Record

* **Explanation** – The statement for the record can be offered both
on the floor and during committee proceedings (See Advocacy
Ask #22). Many committees will accept statements from the public for the record. At a hearing, a committee member will request
that the statement be included in the hearing record. You can submit a statement as an individual or as part of your organization.

* **Why It Is Helpful** – Your statement will indicate exactly how a
specific piece of legislation or agency action could hurt your issue or organization. Or, it could discuss how the need for congressional legislation or oversight can help your organization.

* **Tips**

» You should clearly articulate your thoughts on a proposed
piece of legislation, regulation, or policy.

» Include your background as an explanation about why you
are an expert on the issue.

» Your statement for the record should not exceed ten pages,
but try to be as concise as possible. You should also include
a cover letter or header that includes the name of the committee, the date on which the hearing took place, and the
hearing topic. It should also have your name, title, organization, and city.

» Bonus tip: Committee staffers have to find a member of
Congress to submit your statement for the record. Work to
identify a member of the committee who will attend the
hearing, offer the statement for the record, and share that
information.

43. Field Hearings

* **Explanation** – Hearings that are not held on Capitol Hill are often
referred to as "Field Hearings." They are held for many reasons,

commonly in order to go to the source or the scene of a major national issue. This will then raise awareness of an issue and evaluate programs at the specific place the issue is most prominent. Generally, the field hearings are similar in formalities and procedures to those that take place in Washington D.C. The location of the field hearing varies based on needs and Members' requests.

- **Why They Are Helpful** – These hearings are helpful because they allow those close to the issue to voice their opinions and concerns directly to the committee. This also results in increased media attention for the issues, which can provide a number of benefits to the individuals and organizations involved. The public is given an opportunity to ask questions and hear responses from the committee. You can request or ask your member of Congress to hold a field hearing in your community. You can also ask if any upcoming field hearings are already scheduled nearby.

- **Tips**
  - » Be prepared to explain what topics you would like the field hearing to cover.
  - » You can also suggest potential witnesses to testify at the field hearing.
  - » Also, suggest potential field hearing locations within your community.
  - » Even if you or your organization aren't called to testify, you can still attend the field hearings. Remember, while these hearings are public, there may be limited space.
  - » Also remember that congressional hearings are very formal, even field hearings. When attending a hearing, avoid public disruptions such as applause or other interruptions.

44. Government Accountability Office (GAO) Investigation

- **Explanation** – The Government Accountability Office (GAO) can conduct investigations at the request of Congress. The basis of the request is almost always potential mismanagement, waste, fraud, abuse, or some other inappropriate activity in the exercise of federal authority. GAO is a nonpartisan agency working directly for Congress. They respond to congressional requests for testimony and have the goal of allowing Congress to work more efficiently. Congressional mandates are given highest priority for their investigations, followed by committee Member requests, and then individual congressional Member requests.

- **Why Is It Helpful** – The GAO is designed to hold federal programs accountable. The GAO can increase federal efficiency and government credibility. Citizens can write to congressional committees to request and explain why a GAO investigation is necessary. All requests for GAO reports will come from a congressional committee or from a Member of Congress.

- **Tips**
    - » All previous GAO reports are available on their website www.gao.gov, unless they are classified or sensitive.
    - » You can find out which Member of Congress requested a congressional investigation by checking the appendix of GAO reports and sometimes the introductions of the reports.
    - » GAO responds to media requests only minimally during the course of an investigation; however, media can be referred to the specific Member of Congress who initiated the request.
    - » While a committee Member must make the investigative request, anyone can report abuse or fraud within federal programs by emailing them at fraudnet@gao.gov or calling them at 1-800-424-5454.

45. Introduce Legislation

- **Explanation** – While only Members of Congress can introduce a bill, anyone can introduce the idea of a piece of legislation to their respective member of Congress. A request to introduce legislation typically involves scheduling a meeting with your Member of Congress because this can be the most effective method of persuasion. However, additional information will likely be requested of you; some of it may require written documents. If you can convince your Member of Congress that the bill should be introduced to Congress for the good of her constituents, then it is possible that she will so.

- **Why It Is Helpful** – Citizens shape, recommend, and advocate for laws by going through members of Congress. This means that the issues most prevalent within your community or organization can be addressed by everyday citizens and not just those who are elected or have vast resources.

- Tips
  - » Make sure you have thoroughly evaluated the need for a piece of legislation introduced to impact your issues. Too often advocates want a bill introduced, only to learn after its introduction that you need something completely different.
  - » If you have the background, you can attempt to write a first draft of a bill, but that is not necessary. Moreover, your draft of a bill is not likely to be what gets introduced.
  - » Be prepared to be persistent. Members of Congress are asked to introduce bills often, but they understand that there are better, more efficient advocacy asks to help push an issue along.
  - » Talk about your personal connection to the issue and position yourself as an expert. Offer to help with the marathon of support and coalitions that start after a bill is introduced.

46. Co-sponsor Legislation

- **Explanation** – While only one original sponsor is allowed on a bill, multiple co-sponsors can be added to a bill. Members of Congress can sponsor a bill both when it is first introduced as an original co-sponsor, and again after it is introduced as a co-sponsor. An unlimited number of co-sponsors are allowed. The names of the cosponsors are submitted with the bill. Sponsors of the bill seek support in various ways. Members of Congress often ask for co-sponsors through a "Dear Colleague" letter (See Dear Colleague Advocacy Ask).
- **Why Is It Helpful** – If you advocate for a bill, you can work to convince your Member of Congress to co-sponsor it. The more cosponsors a bill has, the more likely it is to raise awareness about an issue.
- Tips
  - » When convincing your Member of Congress to co-sponsor a bill, you should discuss why it is important and how it will impact the Member's constituents.
  - » You can view the bills and their sponsors and cosponsors at www.congress.gov
  - » While many co-sponsors on a bill are good, no amount of co-sponsors will guarantee that your bill will become law.

47. Testifying as a Hearing Witness

- **Explanation** – Congressional committees hold numerous hearings throughout the year. These hearings require witnesses to come and testify to share their expertise with Congress. When you testify as a witness, you will likely need to file a written copy of your testimony to the committee in advance. Then, oral testimony will be presented at the hearing. After you provide testimony, there is a question and answer period between you and the members of the committee.
- **Why It Is Helpful** – If chosen as a congressional hearing witness, you will have one of the biggest stages to share your issues and concerns with the nation and the world. Hearings can cover a myriad of topics at a high level or with very specific and niche topics. For many industries, these hearings can help to reaffirm or establish an individual's or organization's expertise on a particular topic.
- **Tips**
    - » Testimony must typically be filed 24-48 hours in advance of the hearing.
    - » The testimony will be submitted electronically and later published online.
    - » In rare instances, the committees can choose not to require a written testimony if the witness is invited without enough advance notice.
    - » Each committee member is generally allowed to question the witness for up to five minutes. If requested, additional time may be permitted.

ABOUT THE AUTHOR

Best-selling author, acclaimed speaker, and advisor Nicole Tisdale works with individuals and organizations across the United States who are eager to accelerate policy issues, increase advocacy efforts, and create changes in their communities. During her tenure on the Capitol Hill, Nicole has represented the U.S. and Department of State to more than 30 nations, negotiating a range of security, economic, intelligence, and human rights issues with foreign leaders. She is a respected collaborator, known for her winning record of developing and executing bipartisan agendas.

After serving on Capitol Hill for a decade, Nicole founded Advocacy Blueprints, a company focused on Congressional trainings and consulting. Advocacy Blueprints provides a variety of customized courses, seminars, workshops, and consultations for government entities (federal, state, territorial, local and tribal), corporations, associations, and individual clients. Advocacy Blueprints brings a variety of proven advocacy tools and techniques to assist clients with building and improving their government affairs programs, preparing and delivering congressional testimonies and briefings, and the design and development of strategies for building effective relationships and policies in Congress.

She received both her Juris Doctorate ('09) and Bachelors of Art ('06) from the University of Mississippi. She is a frustrated golfer who enjoys entertaining in her home.

Contact Nicole at nicole@nicoletisdale.com to inquire about having her work with your organization or speak at your event.

Free Bonus materials are also available at www.nicoletisdale.com.

Made in the USA
Coppell, TX
25 February 2023